Managing
the State

The MIT Press
Cambridge, Massachusetts,
and London, England

Managing
the State

Martha Wagner Weinberg

This book was set in IBM Composer Baskerville
by Techdata Associates
printed on R & E Book,
and bound in Columbia Milbank MBL 4974
by Colonial Press Inc.
in the United States of America

Library of Congress Cataloging in Publication
Data

Weinberg, Martha Wagner.
    Managing the State.

    Bibliography: p.
    Includes index.
    1. Massachusetts—Governors. 2. Massachu-
setts—Executive departments—Management.
3. Sargent, Francis W., 1915-   I. Title.
JK3152 1969.W45   353.9′744′0313   76-50628
ISBN 0-262-23077-1 (hardcover)
        0-262-73048-0 (paperback)

Contents

Preface
ix

1
Introduction
1

2
The Governor
as Public Manager
15

3
Gubernatorial Style
in Managing the State
43

4
The Department of Public Works
75

5

The Department
of Public Welfare
107

6

The Massachusetts
Housing Finance Agency
147

7

The Department
of Mental Health
177

8

Conclusions
207

Selected Bibliography
233

Index
237

Preface

This book grew out of my experience working in executive offices in two states, Illinois and Massachusetts. Like many other young people who worked for government in the late 1960s and early 1970s, I was extremely optimistic about government's ability to produce and implement policies that would improve citizens' lives. The focus of this optimism for me, as it was for others, was the chief executive. In cities and states around the country progressive, intelligent mayors and governors became for many people the symbolic embodiment of these hopes and the reference point for gauging our successes and failures.

The two governors for whom I worked, Richard Ogilvie and Francis Sargent, were bright, honest, and highly motivated men. Though each can point to a significant number of impressive achievements during his term, neither they nor other chief executives like them were able to provide the kind of wholesale salvation through enlightened leadership for which many people had unrealistically hoped. The question that was foremost in my mind as I left the government was why there was such a great discrepancy between what we had come to expect from governors and what they actually are able to do. It became clear to me that perhaps the most important reason for this discrepancy is that very few people understand what kinds of problems governors face and what the constraints are that are imposed on those who work in the public sector. Because the question had both personal and intellectual significance for me, I decided to look back at my experience in Massachusetts and to ask, during the Sargent years, what it meant to manage the state.

When I began this study, I did it still believing that the profession of government is basically an honorable one, worthy of study and effort. I am grateful to the many government employees with whom I dealt in Massachusetts state government who reaffirmed this belief for me in the course of my work and who generously and thoughtfully helped me try to figure out what makes state government perform as it does. Much of the material in this study is based on information gathered in interviews with state employees, which I conducted over a one-and-one-half-year period. Many of these persons asked to remain un-named. Quotations from all those interviewed are based on notes in my possession.

Alan Altshuler, Samuel Beer, Lawrence Brown, John Russell, and Robert Weinberg read drafts of this study and provided me with many valuable suggestions about how to improve it. I am especially indebted to James Q. Wilson, an inspiring teacher and the supervisor of the doctoral dissertation on which this book is based, and to Jeffrey Pressman, who reviewed the entire manuscript and provided encouragement and excellent advice during my first year of teaching at M.I.T. Gail Lopata and Nelle Wagner were enormously helpful in the production of the manuscript, and I benefited a great deal from their support.

Managing
the State

1
Introduction

On the day that a governor assumes his office, he becomes many things to many people. As he sits down behind his desk, his own primary concern may be with trying to figure out how to formulate and implement some specific public policies, assemble resources, and survive. However, his own criteria for success or failure may bear little resemblance to those of the electorate who will eventually judge his performance. How one evaluates a publicly elected chief executive depends as much on the evaluator's perspective as it does on the number or kinds of policies for which that executive is responsible. A journalist or television commentator may view the man in the corner office primarily as a source of public entertainment, a focus for public respect or disdain, a potential star or media failure. A businessman or private sector executive may see the official quite differently. For him, the governor may be the symbol of an increasingly powerful public presence in the private sector, a force that has an important impact on the environment and financial condition of the economy. His criterion for evaluating the success of the governor may be whether he can keep taxes from increasing, stimulate business, and prevent public interference in the private sector.

To a state legislator or politician, the governor, as an important representative of a party, a policy, or a program, may symbolize an entirely different set of issues. As he evaluates the governor, the questions he asks of him may be how well he recognizes and rewards his friends and how sensitive he is to the political climate. These criteria for evaluating a governor may be diametrically opposed to those of a citizen or a constituent, who may perceive the chief executive as a duly elected public figure whose job is to provide government services and programs to citizens who want or need them.

Although they may never agree on what makes a governor a "good" chief executive or on *how* the state should be managed, all of these people have a stake in understanding the governor's capacity for managing the state. For those citizens who care about one specific or narrow issue with which state government deals, understanding how that issue gets on government's agenda and what happens to it from that point on may provide the basis for a feasible strategy for action. To them the question of what managing the state means may be put in very specific and immediate terms. Can a new center for mentally retarded children be built and what can a governor do about it? How can a group of citizens persuade a chief executive that he should oppose the building of a highway, and what incentives are there for him to be on their side of the issue? Who will make the decision to keep or to cut medical assistance payments to the poor, and how can a chief executive influence such a decision? The answers to these questions become crucial for any group of citizens or activists who want to achieve some specific end.

The electorate also has a stake in understanding how the state is managed. One of the basic assumptions of American democratic theory is that the electorate is able to influence public policy by choosing a chief executive who is willing and able to control the policies and behavior of his subordinates, ensuring government's responsiveness and responsibility to the public. In fact, governors do not always control their agencies. At times they do not wish to control them. They often have no clear idea of the public's or their own policy agenda. Instead of controlling and managing all agencies in an even-handed manner, their interest in agencies and their resources to control them vary. They attempt to enforce their own policy preferences on some agencies with little success; and they never deal with other agencies, even though these agencies may behave exactly the way the chief executive would like. Often it may be far more important to them to concentrate their efforts on appearing to be in control, on cultivating a public image of a management style that seems to please and to soothe the electorate and on formulating large numbers of new programs that may never be implemented but that give the appearance of activity and initiative. In addition, contrary to what democratic theory would lead us to believe, it is clear that the preferences of specialized bureaucrats often dominate the choice of policies and the outcome of issues with or without the consent of the elected or appointed generalists to whom in theory they are accountable.

By examining closely what public sector management means, citizens can gain two important advantages. They can, if they wish, use such an analysis to help them construct a more realistic set of criteria for evaluating a governor than the simplistic one of whether things seem to be under control. In addition, in the process of looking at how governors make decisions and how public policies are made, it becomes clear that there are many points in the political process where individuals can and do influence government's behavior. Understanding where these points are and when and where citizens, elected representatives, and governors have access to them can be a powerful lever to use in moving the government.

The study of gubernatorial management and leadership is important not only to the electorate and to specialized publics who receive tangible benefits from the state but also to scholars who try to understand why government behaves the way it does. For the most part political scientists who have dealt with chief executives have concentrated their attention on their formal authority and powers. Their studies have focused primarily on the role chief executives play in the political structure and typically have neglected the question of how chief executives can influence the climate of the jurisdiction over which they preside. The two most notable exceptions to this pattern are the studies of presidential power by Richard Neustadt and James Sterling Young.[1] These books look beyond the executive's formal powers and his position in the political hierarchy and analyze executive leadership at the national level. Neustadt and Young have made it clear that a president's ability to move the government does not necessarily automatically accompany authority and in so doing have raised a whole set of questions that social scientists must answer. If a chief executive wants to accomplish something, what must he do? Why are some executives so much more successful than others? If there is such a thing as political leadership, from where does it come and what difference does it make? What roles do executive "statecraft"[2] and style play in shaping public policy?

Although answering such questions about political executives is a crucial item on the agenda of social scientists, systematic study of them has been limited and has focused almost exclu sively on the chief executive in national government. Little attention has been paid to the states and to gubernatorial leadership, despite the increasingly important questions of public policy that are being decided at the state level. Understanding what managing the state means is of utmost importance to any analyst of public policy. More and more federal funds are passing through state government. It is standard for the rhetoric of political candidates for national office to include promises to promote the "New Federalism," to give states and local governments more responsibility for government programs, and to allow them greater discretion in spending federal monies than they now have. At the same time, governors with increasing frequency are being considered viable candidates for national office. Political analysts argue that their executive experience qualifies them for the most difficult of public management positions. Yet this experience has not been chronicled or studied in any systematic fashion. There is almost no literature on governors and what they do. There has been no significant analysis of how the job of governor compares with the job of other publicly elected chief executives, such as presidents and mayors. Though most analysts would agree that at all levels of government the executive branch is becoming increasingly important in influencing the outcomes of public policy, no one has looked carefully at the questions of what constraints, opportunities, and problems all chief executives face or of how they differ from each other.

The Focus

This is a study of one governor's management of the state agencies for which he was responsible. It necessarily has a dual focus—on the governor, Francis Sargent of Massachusetts, and on several of the agencies he managed. To understand executive leadership and management, it is necessary to look at both the governor's style and immediate environment and the nature of the agencies that are his responsibility. Though the study is not written from the perspective of the journalist, the business executive, the politician, or the constituent, it relies heavily on the insights and cautions characteristic of each. The purpose of the study is to subject to hard scrutiny some of the traditional assumptions about both the governor and the agencies and to analyze the responsibilities and possibilities of managing the state.

The first set of questions this study raises involves the governor. They are aimed at establishing what a publicly elected chief executive *does* to manage the state. Government reformers have often suggested that if only chief executives could perform like the best managers in the private sector and could adopt the latest in business management techniques, government might run more smoothly and effectively.[3] The assumption on which these proposals are based overlooks the fact that a chief executive in the public sector faces different problems from those of the general manager of a private firm. The environment in which he makes decisions is more complex and less controllable than that of the private sector executive. His term is limited. He shares power and responsibility with many people. The important question to ask is not why a governor does not behave like a private sector executive, but what the significant differences are between public and private sector management. What does management of a large bureaucracy in a political setting mean? What criteria does a governor employ to decide which policy choices are "better" or "worse" than others?

Distinguishing between how an elected chief executive differs from his private sector counterpart is a necessary first step in understanding what managing the state means. In addition, it is necessary to ask how chief executives make decisions. Analysts of public sector decisions have drawn heavily on two models to explain how policymakers behave. The first might be called the "rational policymaker" model.[4] This model assumes that in many cases decisionmakers consciously factor problems into their component parts, making them more subject to conscious management than they would be if they remained aggregated. Further, it suggests it is desirable and possible for the decision-maker to analyze the values at stake in a given problem and to assign some priorities in arriving at their solution on the basis of the values that these problems raise. The implication of this school of thought is that executives for many problems can and do ask three questions: What am I trying to do? How can I do it? How will I know when I have done it? The model has been used prescriptively as well as analytically. Though few contemporary writers who advocate this style of decision making would argue that it can be applied comprehensively or in all situations, many people who advise public agencies argue that this rational ordering of priorities and the ability to plan that it implies are possible and desirable for political executives.

The alternative model of decision making is perhaps best typified by the theory of Charles Lindblom, who argues that decision making in government can best be characterized not as a rational process but, instead, as "muddling through."[5] He suggests that decisionmakers make only incremental changes in the policy process by continually modifying the current situation. He argues that they do this by making a series of "successive limited comparisons," which always result in marginal adjustment of policies and involve little long-range calculation, planning, or ranking of objectives.

Although both theories provide useful clues to executive decision making, neither is adequate to explain how elected chief executives make decisions. To understand the dynamics of executive leadership, it is necessary to raise the level of argument beyond considering which of the two models is more correct and to ask what executives consider when they make specific decisions. This study shows that governors respond to crises, to those issues and incidents they perceive as significant in influencing their political and administrative success. At times they respond after having made a highly sophisticated and tightly rational calculation of costs and benefits. In other instances they seem to be prototypes of the decisionmaker who "muddles through." To understand why this apparent disparity exists, one must ask not only whether chief executives do or do not calculate their decisions, but a series of additional questions as well. Where do a governor's ideas on policy making come from? How does an issue become political? Why is political crisis so important in determining how a chief executive formulates and executes public policy? Why does he take action on certain administrative issues and not on others?

To understand fully what the answers to these questions explain, it is necessary to focus on the governor himself and on his immediate environment. Chief executives do not all behave the same way. Their styles, their use of resources, and the extent of their cultivation of certain kinds of policies and issues vary from governor to governor and from state to state. To understand why this is true and how it affects policy outcomes requires that we ask an additional set of questions about chief executives. What other functions does a governor have to perform? How does an issue get on his agenda? What resources does he have to affect a particular situation? What agencies does he try to control and why? What do his attempts to change an agency's behavior or to make the agency perform as he wishes cost him?

The second major focus of this study is on the agencies themselves, on the public bureaucracy for which the chief executive is responsible. To understand what managing the state means, one must look not only at "the manager" but also at "the managed." The single most striking feature about public agencies is that they differ greatly in their susceptibility to gubernatorial control. There are several reasons for this. Public sector agencies with extremely complicated and often contradictory agendas that can be influenced by many different constituencies may behave very differently from organizations in either the public or the private sector that have a clear cut, sharply defined mandate. What an agency's agenda is and who sets it is an important dimension along which agencies differ. In addition, the degree of complexity of the subject matter with which agencies deal also influences the extent to which they can be managed or controlled.[6] An agency that has responsibility for "the welfare problem" or for the complicated issue of mental health may be less amenable to control than an agency such as a department of public works whose mandate is to build highways.

The differences among agencies in terms of their susceptibility to gubernatorial control can also be explained by the differences in their organizational structure. Each public agency has its own history and style, traditions and norms, which affect both how well it functions and how accountable and responsive it is to the chief executive.[7] It is therefore necessary to examine each organization's distinct personality in some detail to understand the degree to which it does or does not respond to the governor. For each agency it is important to know, to the extent that the governor himself does not set agency agendas, who does. Who are the agency's natural constituents and how do their policy preferences differ from or correspond to those of the chief executive? To what extent is the governor's ability to manage the agency a function of traits peculiar to individual organizations?

The two central questions of this study reflect the need to look at both the governor and the agencies. The first of these is the question of whether and why the governor tries to control a particular agency. Control implies his ability not only to have the agency respond in a manner satisfactory to him, but also to make an agency change its behavior to reflect his preferences at some cost in political resources to him. In addition, it is necessary to ask whether the agencies behave in the way the governor would prefer and why this is true. There are some public bureaucracies that seem to be immune to gubernatorial management, even if the governor decides to spend substantial time and effort in managing them. Still others behave in a manner satisfactory to both the public and the chief executive with little or no coaxing. Speculation on why this happens is crucial to understanding both what we can expect from political leaders and what areas of the political process need closer scrutiny.

The Setting

This book is a study of Francis Sargent's management of Massachusetts government from 1969, when he became acting governor, until 1974, when he was defeated in his bid for reelection. The study focuses on Sargent and on Massachusetts for several reasons. Massachusetts is a large industrial state with a tradition of professional government service. Although the Democratic party has traditionally won most of the state's lower constitutional offices, competition between Republican and Democratic candidates for the office of governor has always involved spirited and often highly personalized politics. Individual personalities and issues have had greater salience than party label in gubernatorial elections.

Sargent was an especially interesting governor to look at because he represented a paradox. In November of 1974, he was defeated in his bid for reelection by a Democrat, Michael Dukakis, whose primary charge against Sargent was that he had not managed the government well. Yet Sargent was one of only a handful of state chief executives in the United States whose career before becoming governor had been spent as a manager of various administrative agencies. Both his experience as an executive in a public bureaucracy and his own early stated strong feelings about making government more manageable might lead one to believe that the management of government should have been one issue on which he might not have been vulnerable. Yet he was soundly defeated in a campaign characterized by a great deal of debate about how well the government was running. Why this occurred requires a closer look at both what management meant to the public and how specific agencies were performing, in response to the governor's demands and to other pressures on them.

Instead of looking at all of the agencies for which Sargent was nominally responsible, this book focuses on four—the Department of Public Works, the Department of Public Welfare, the Massachusetts Housing Finance Agency, and the Department of Mental Health. One of the basic assumptions of this study is that all agencies are not alike, that organizations, like individuals, have distinct personalities that are the result of their own particular history, their legal mandate and their mission, their professionalism, and a variety of other factors. Therefore, to make general statements about a governor and his relationship to his agencies as if those agencies were interchangeable is a meaningless exercise. This study looks at four agencies in some detail in hopes of better understanding how a governor's ability to manage them varies and how one agency differs from another.

The two most significant variables in selecting agencies to analyze in this study were whether or not the governor tried to affect a particular agency and whether or not the agency produced policies in keeping with his wishes or preferences. These two variables are crucial in understanding how chief executives manage their agencies. The rhetoric of political campaigns might lead one to believe that if an executive is intelligent and competent, he manages all of his agencies all of the time. In fact, anyone who has worked in a political hierarchy or who has observed politics closely knows that some agencies that a governor desperately wants to control are beyond his reach. Other agencies produce outcomes in keeping with his wishes and they receive no attention from the governor whatsoever. Still others operate almost independently of the chief executive, receiving no attention or direction from the governor and making policy on their own, with no regard to whether the governor approves of that policy. Not all gubernatorial efforts at management are successful and governors are often labeled successful managers of agencies they make no attempts to manage.

On the basis of these two variables, gubernatorial intervention and agency response, it is possible to draw a four-cell table and insert four Massachusetts agencies.

	Gets preferred response	Does not get preferred response
Governor tries to control	Department of Public Works	Department of Public Welfare
Governor does not try to control	Massachusetts Housing Finance Agency	Department of Mental Health

The agencies were selected for three reasons. Each of the agencies selected differed along dimensions crucial to the typology and fit into a different cell of the table when they were studied. They were also different from each other in the nature and clarity of their central mission, in size, and in organizational structure. Finally, I had easy access to the personnel and data in all four agencies and some personal experience in working with two, the Department of Public Welfare and the Department of Mental Health.

What affected the behavior of these agencies and their response to Sargent is spelled out in this study. An analysis of four other agencies would have produced different narratives and different sets of issues at stake during the Sargent administration. This study is not meant to be a comprehensive catalog of all agencies of state government. One of its underlying assumptions is that to understand the entire state bureaucracy it is necessary to understand several individual agencies well. Other agencies that fit into the table could have been substituted. What is important is that those organizations studied should be studied in some detail. At times Sargent and the four agencies seem to defy drawing any general conclusions. However, in addition to detailing the Massachusetts example, this study raises general questions one might want to ask of governors and their agencies in all states. What does management mean for a publicly elected chief executive? What accounts for variations in style, in use of resources, and in levels of success among governors? To whom are agencies really accountable and responsive? Where do their norms and goals come from? To what extent is public policy public and controllable?

This study began by cautioning that governors are many things to many people. They are important symbols. They can be leaders. They can also fail or succeed at influencing public policy. Some are characterized as strong, others as weak. But even taking into account the many criteria by which they can be judged and the variation among them, at least two things are clear. Neither their behavior nor that of the agencies for which they are responsible is random. And though the catalysts for and controls on that behavior are often difficult to distinguish, the results have a major impact on large numbers of citizens in terms of who receives tangible and important public goods. This book seeks to analyze the dynamics of executive control and its effects on public sector agencies.

Notes

1

See Richard Neustadt, *Presidential Power* and James Sterling Young, *The Washington Community 1800-1828.*

2

The term is Young's, *The Washington Community 1800-1828.*

3

See, for example, the Commission on Organization of the Executive Branch of Government, "General Management of the Executive Branch." This was known as the first Hoover Commission report.

4

Typical of the applications of this model are works like Marshall Dimock's *A Philosophy of Administration* and Charles Hitch and Roland McKean's *The Economics of Defense in the Nuclear Age.* Though it represents highly refined use of this theory in its stress on efficiency and "satisficing," perhaps the classic statement of the rational model is Herbert Simon's *Administrative Behavior.*

5

See Charles Lindblom, "The Science of Muddling Through," in *Public Administration.* Although Lindblom and others have written more extensively on this subject, this is the most concise statement of this theory.

6

Richard Fenno has made this same point in writing about congressional committees in his articles on the House Appropriations Committee, "The House Appropriations Committee as a Political System: The Problem of Integration" and the House Committee on Education and Labor, "The House Committee on Education and Labor." He points out the importance of the subject matter with which the two committees deal in determining how they function. I am grateful to Jeffrey Pressman for pointing out the usefulness of Fenno's studies in explaining agency behavior.

7

The importance of these differences is well established in the literature on large organizations. James Q. Wilson's *Varieties of Police Behavior* is one of the best studies that has been done on the importance of structure and ethos in influencing the performance of large organizations.

2

**The Governor
as Public Manager**

In 1969 when Francis W. Sargent assumed the governorship of Massachusetts, he became, by virtue of his office, the chief manager of the state. As chief executive he was to preside over a budget of approximately $3 billion and an organization of more than sixty-five thousand employees. Even compared to large private sector businesses, such an operation was enormous. If the Commonwealth of Massachusetts were a private firm, it would rank ahead of such corporate giants as General Foods and Standard Oil of California in number of employees. But Sargent could not manage Massachusetts as if he were managing a private firm of comparable size. Unlike most private sector executives, he had a short fixed term of office. In addition, many of the parts of the organization over which he presided were, by virtue of their being public, responsive to constituencies, citizen groups, and pressures over which he had no control. Though all publicly elected chief executives are faced with a long list of things they "ought" to do, they step into a situation for which there is almost no guidance on how to accomplish it. One of the first issues they have to face is what management of the state means and what strategies they can use to manage those issues that are important to them.

Sargent was not a newcomer to public service. He was elected to his first full term as governor in 1970, after having stepped up to be acting governor from the position of lieutenant governor when Governor John Volpe left Massachusetts to become Secretary of Transportation in the Nixon administration. Though an architect by training and the proprietor of a sporting goods store on Cape Cod, he had spent most of his life in public service as a bureaucrat. From 1947 until 1965, he worked in various state and federal agencies in the field of natural resources, serving as the commissioner of the Department of Natural Resources from 1956 until 1959. In 1959 he accepted a job as executive director of the United States Outdoor Recreation Resources Review Commission in Washington. He returned to Massachusetts in 1963, when he joined the staff of the Department of Public Works. In 1965, he became commissioner of the Department of Public Works, the job he had until he resigned in 1966 to run on the Republican ticket for lieutenant governor with John Volpe. In 1970, he defeated Mayor Kevin White of Boston by more than 350,000 votes to win his first full term as governor.

Sargent's choice and deployment of staff reflected his style of management and had far-reaching consequences for the policies of his administration. Sargent brought with him into the governor's office two men who had been with him since his days in the Department of Natural Resources. Robert Yasi, a lawyer and Sargent's administrative assistant at the Department of Natural Resources who had worked with Sargent since the 1950s, became chief secretary, the traditional title for the job of the governor's chief of staff. Jack Flannery, a former newsman and disc jockey, was named press secretary. A third longtime friend and colleague of Sargent's, Donald Dwight, was named commissioner of administration and finance when Sargent became acting governor. When Sargent ran for his first full term, he picked Dwight to run for lieutenant governor on the ticket with him. To round out the inner circle of his key advisors, Sargent appointed as his urban affairs advisor Albert Kramer, a young, liberal lawyer who had previously been a state representative and one of the founders of the Massachusetts Law Reform Institute. Kramer had also worked with Sargent at the Department of Public Works. After the 1970 election Sargent promoted Kramer to the newly created job of chief of policy and programs.

Sargent relied exclusively on men whom he already knew and with whom he had previously worked to fill the major positions in his office. During the course of Sargent's tenure as governor, these people were to remain the key actors on the Sargent staff, though there was some shuffling of personnel and tasks. Dwight was less frequently consulted as Sargent's term wore on, largely because of the obligations of his own office and because he was

ambitious for a political career of his own. Yasi was named to
the powerful position of commissioner of administration and
finance in 1971. He was neither fond of nor had any particular
aptitude for the job and in 1972 was named to a probate judge-
ship and left the Sargent administration. Jack Flannery in the
meantime became chief secretary. He in turn was replaced as
press secretary by Tom Reardon, a former newsman and member of the state house press corps. It was this group—Yasi,
Flannery, Dwight, Kramer, and Reardon—that formed the core
of the governor's policy staff.

The staff of the governor's office during the Sargent administration included nearly one hundred temporary and permanent
employees. About forty of these people held professional positions. The staff was approximately the same size as those of the
two previous governors, John Volpe and Endicott Peabody.
Many of the titles and divisions of the governor's office have
been the same for many years, including the positions of chief
secretary and legal counsel, and the offices of State Service, the
Governor's Office of Service, and the Governor's Appointments
Office. All of these offices were the responsibility of a senior
staff member and functioned almost like small agencies in themselves. For example, the Governor's State Service Office answered or referred all correspondence sent to the governor. The
Governor's Appointments Office had a staff of five and was
concerned with the governor's schedule. The head of this office
also served as the chief liaison to the Republican party and to
the Sargent campaign organization until the few months before
the primaries and the election. The Governor's Office of State
Service, traditionally the arm of the governor's office that dis-
pensed patronage and supervised all jobs, was headed in the last
half of the Sargent administration by a personnel professional,
Robert Dumont, who had previously been the vice-president for
personnel of a large Boston-based insurance company. Dumont
had a staff of ten people and concerned himself almost entirely
with recruitment of high-level personnel and with the hundreds
of appointments to boards and commissions that the governor

had to make each year. Sargent's legal counsel, William Young, had a staff of two lawyers whose primary function was to handle legal matters immediately involving the governor. They also provided a limited amount of legal advice for administrative agencies.

The press office that Reardon headed was small. He devoted much of his time to assisting the state house press corps and to general policy matters. The legislative secretary to the governor, William Morrow, a former state representative from Haverhill, had a staff of two whose primary function was to track bills through the legislature and to persuade legislators to act in accordance with the governor's wishes.

In addition to these long standing positions within the governor's office, Sargent had a policy staff whose composition and structure varied considerably during his tenure as governor. Headed by Kramer, and with Stephen Teichner and John Drew serving as back-up policy generalists and seconds-in-command, this staff consisted of from ten to twenty persons who specialized in functional policy areas or who were assigned specific agencies to monitor. In 1974 the average age of these staff people was twenty-eight and their average tenure in their jobs was approximately one and one-half years. More than half of them had been trained as lawyers, but very few came to their jobs with any previous experience in government or in the substantive area that they were supposed to monitor. Their jobs were almost entirely self-defined. None of them had any staff of their own except for any informal help they could get from the agencies with which they dealt. Because of the broad and undefined mandate under which they operated, they generally could pick and choose the issues with which they dealt, though at times either Kramer or crisis dictated what their jobs were. The issues and agencies covered by this staff consequently varied greatly during the Sargent administration and were highly dependent on what issues were politically important and on the personal inclinations of the staff involved.

Executive Management of Public Agencies

To a certain extent the management style of the Sargent administration was determined by Sargent's own personality and background, his choice of staff, and their assignments. But managing
the state also involved implicitly or explicitly choosing strategies, devoting energy and resources to some tasks and not to
others, and maintaining some consistency in policies and programs. In facing this issue, Sargent, like other elected chief executives, was faced with a paradox. The electorate and various
constituencies would arrive at some notion about whether he
had been a successful manager. Because of this fact, and because
of the instrumental importance that it might have in achieving
policies important to him, management had to be a serious consideration throughout his tenure in office. But for Sargent, like
other elected chief executives, it was not clear when he took office what management meant, how he could learn it, or what
measures of success or failure he could apply to his efforts.

For years, government reformers have urged political executives to take their cues on how to manage from the private sector. The most simple-minded recommendations of this kind
have urged chief executives to adopt wholesale a "rational" approach to management, which includes regulating the executive's span of control, integrating functions, tightening formal
lines of authority, and giving a great deal of attention to long-
range planning.[1] Such strategies do not take into account the
fact that reallocation of formal authority and reorganization of
functions do not necessarily change the substance of government operations. Though rhetorically pleasing, recommendations that organizations be more rationally structured have
proved ineffective as ways of controlling and managing public
sector organizations and private sector organizations with complicated environments and agendas.

It is not fair to discard all private sector organization theory
as inapplicable to the public sector simply because the "conventional wisdom" of reform and reorganization of large organiza-

tions is not useful. A more significant obstacle to a governor's taking his cues on management from business theory is that the publicly elected chief executive has no counterpart in the private sector. There has been a great deal of useful literature written in the field of management about the job of the general manager or about the private sector executive.[2] However, even the most perceptive and thoroughly argued of these studies, though useful in some of the insights that they provide into any responsible official's job, do not describe the kind of situation into which Francis Sargent stepped when he became governor or exactly what he would have to do to manage the state.

In seeking a private sector analog to the publicly elected chief executive, one might look first at the "general manager," the chief operating officer of a firm. According to Kenneth Andrews, the general manager's responsibilities include supervising current operations, planning future operations, coordinating the functions and capabilities of the organization, and making a distinct personal contribution to the business.[3] Like a governor, according to Andrews, a general manager "does not so much make as recognize, ratify or be made captive by decisions emerging out of powerful organizational processes not easily interpreted."[4] The general manager, like the public sector executive, is therefore not at all times in complete control of all decisions made in his organization. But the climate in which the governor operates is different in many other respects from that of the general manager. Andrews suggests that one of the ways a general manager makes his greatest impact on an organization is by knowing what specialists he needs throughout the organization, hiring them, and coordinating their input. Governors, unlike general managers, often have extremely limited control over the hiring and firing of personnel, especially in states with strong civil service systems and tight ties between the legislature and the bureaucracy. In addition, though a general manager has to weigh possible costs against benefits in arriving at a strategy, he generally does so with some firm notion of an "acceptable level of risk."[5] For a governor, this acceptable level of risk is much more difficult to define, both because of the unpredictability of crisis situations and of public response to them and because of the limits of his control over other political actors in the political arena. Finally, one could argue that any elected chief executive presides over a variety of kinds of functions, including provision of services, regulation, income transfer, and adjudication, far more widespread and diverse than those of most general managers and that this fact alone makes the jobs of the two not comparable. Perhaps, then, a more appropriate private sector analogy might be to the private sector executive, the person ultimately *responsible* for the performance of the firm.

In describing the job of the executive, both Chester Barnard and Philip Selznick have gone beyond the assumption that executives give orders that are instantly obeyed.[6] Both argue that the primary goal of all executives, private or public, is organizational maintenance, which they manage by offering a series of incentives to those associated with the firm. Barnard stresses the fact that all organizations are different and that these incentives have to be tied to the particular purposes and resources of the organization the executive is trying to manage. Selznick carries this theory further by arguing that the success of a large organization depends heavily on the extent to which that organization has a sense of "distinctive competence," a clear sense of mission with which the incentives offered by the organization are congruent.

But a governor's job is even more complex than that of Barnard's and Selznick's executives. The theories of Selznick and Barnard, as far as they go, are useful in understanding what governors do. Like his private sector counterpart, a publicly elected executive must understand the differences among the large organizations for which he is responsible. One of the primary goals of his management must be organizational maintenance. But a governor must be equally concerned with another kind of maintenance, maintenance of his own tenuous position as an elected official. Unlike his private sector counterpart, he has to be reelected at least every four years. His full attention cannot be devoted to the functioning of his administrative apparatus. Although like a private sector executive he must try to set objectives for his organization, he must do it in a far more complex environment in which he shares jurisdiction over the agenda with many others. In addition, public sector executives have far fewer measures of ongoing success than most private sector executives. At times, they are assumed to be responsible for issues over which they have no control. Their autonomy to act is considerably more tightly circumscribed than that of private executives. They often have to share jurisdiction with other public institutions such as the courts and the legislature at the state level. They also are often helpless to act in the federal system and must try to make policy on issues over which the federal government and/or local governments have significant influence. Governors and all public political officials also have to share public powers with private actors, who may be extremely influential and, at the same time, subject to little public scrutiny or control. In addition, a governor is often perceived to be responsible for events (such as inflation, for example) that are beyond the bounds of his jurisdiction or for having to forgo redistributive policies that would benefit individual citizens in order to allow his state to remain economically competitive with other jurisdictions.

Though many of the cautions and insights of the literature on management of private sector agencies are useful in clarifying some aspects of the public sector executive's job, it is clear that a newly elected chief executive cannot generalize about his job on the basis of familiarity with the private sector. The setting is different; the constraints on him are different; and the measures of success or failure are different. It is therefore necessary to look at what managing the state means for a governor from a fresh perspective, to ask what tasks "management" implies.

Implicit in the frequent call for chief executives to manage their agencies effectively is the assumption that "running agencies" is one task and that it involves one set of procedures or at least some common denominator that calls for a single coherent philosophy or style of administration. Although a comprehensive and consistent style of management may be important in determining how well a government or one particular administration performs, the rubric of "managing the bureaucracy" covers a variety of kinds of issues and problems which, in turn, require a variety of skills, talents, and resources. Handling "managerial issues" for a governor may involve his or his staff's performing a whole series of functions, some of which they may enjoy and handle well, while they show little talent or inclination for others. These include such jobs as

— changing or initiating policy
— maintaining a policy or a position under pressure
— setting a tone and keeping morale high
— mediating disputes among different agencies or factions within agencies
— marketing
— recruiting
— allocating resources.

In addition, a governor's ability to "manage" an agency may be judged by whether or not the agency behaves as the governor would like it to behave. In some situations the agency performs as the governor would like it to perform although he uses no resources to ensure that this happens. In this situation the agency "complies" with his wishes, whether or not he actively intervenes to ensure that those wishes are carried out. Other managerial situations require that he attempt to achieve "control" over an agency, that is, that he use scarce resources to change the behavior of the agency to make it behave as he would like. Gaining compliance or "control" may involve two entirely different strategies and styles of management.

Francis Sargent had no overriding philosophy of management or strategy for running the large agencies that fell under his jurisdiction. He describes himself as a pragmatist, handling each issue as it came up, deciding it on its merits, and then standing firm on his decisions.[7] He considered such issues as the reorganization of state government "unsexy"; and though he worked hard to implement them, his own temperamental inclinations led him to be less interested in the issues of day-to-day management than in crisis issues. He describes himself as the "opposite of the 'Nixon-Richardson prototype.' They would sit down and write memos to plan long-range dealings with the bureaucracy. I don't like memos. I prefer oral arguments, on specific issues on which I can make a decision."[8]

Most of the time Sargent and his staff spent in dealing with agencies was involved with handling "crises," issues, and incidents they felt to be of pressing enough importance to warrant their exclusive attention. Both he and his senior staff members felt that the nature of the governor's job makes it imperative that a major portion of his agenda be dictated by crisis and that for a governor to attempt a long-range management strategy is to attempt to retreat from the unpredictable nature of the problems the governor has to face. Consequently, Sargent surrounded himself with men oriented toward quick action rather than those of a philosophic bent.

If there was any single key staff member who had a conscious, long-range philosophy about how to deal with the agencies responsible to the governor, it was Kramer. This was due more to his intellectual proclivities than to his own philosophy of action because, paradoxically, he was probably more than any other single staff member the source of the office's "crisis orientation." His assessment of the responsiveness of agencies to the governor was pragmatic and did not assume that the relationship between agencies and the chief executive was weighted in favor of the governor. As he put it:

Agencies belong to agencies, not to the governor. When you tamper with the way an agency traditionally operates, you're tampering not only with policy, but with something religious, with the instinct for survival. Few people down in the agencies are willing to kill their own flesh and blood for a "good cause."

They have lots of resources, probably the chief one being the "wearing out factor." They can outlast or wear out any single governor. They'll be there after he's gone. In order to have any control over them, you have to be willing to attack, to give an order, to put your own guys in there. You have to try consciously to seize the resources of the agency, to build a strong patronage system, to cultivate all the loyalties you can. That's the only way you can assure yourself of being able to run anything.[9]

Kramer's insights into overall bureaucratic strategies, lucid though they were, were not the basis of any long-range or conscious effort of his own or of the rest of the staff to put a master plan for administration into effect, however. Though in their handling of a given situation they often consciously or unconsciously acknowledged many of the factors that Kramer cited, the governor and his staff did not claim to have any long-range management objectives or a planning capability. Instead, they felt that most of the energy they put into dealing with the agencies involved handling "what's hot" from day to day.[10]

The ability of all governors and their staffs to manage their agencies depends on their capacity and inclinations to perform many distinct functions well. In order to understand their ability to "run the agencies," it might be useful to examine their style and aptitude for dealing with a variety of management functions.

Changing or Initiating Policy

One of the most easily identifiable management functions for a chief executive is putting in motion a particular policy or taking a stand on an issue or set of procedures that in turn must be implemented by his subordinates in one or more of the administrative agencies. In the Sargent administration, except for instances that involved a highly visible issue or an issue that directly affected the governor's position with the electorate, initiation or change of a policy on the part of the governor's office was largely dependent on the talent, personal inclination, and assignment of the functional policy specialists who worked for Kramer. The result was uneven and depended both on the abilities of the staff person and on the nature and appeal of the issue.

In order to understand the nature of policy initiation or

change, one must understand a crucial characteristic of Sargent's style, namely, that he did not come into office with, nor did he develop, a series of specific policy objectives he was anxious to implement. His consistent *modus operandi* was to pick and choose from among alternatives offered by his staff. This is not to suggest that he had no consistent principles or policies to which he adhered. In fact, he was remarkably steady and unwavering on announced priority policy areas during his tenure in office. However, his style in picking which policies to back was not that of an advocate of his own strong beliefs. Rather, he felt most comfortable having an issue brought before him, hearing out proponents and opponents, then making a decision based on the arguments he heard.

He structured his staff to represent a broad spectrum of political views (as he described them, ranging from "the guy who we suspect is taking orders from Moscow to a few who are *still* trying to impeach Earl Warren"). Kramer and his staff were "liberals," especially on issues of social policy; Flannery and Dwight represented a more conservative perspective. Sargent looked to his staff to provide him with active, lively, and often opposing views from which he could choose a sound position. This was true both on decisions that worked their way up to him and on his own policy initiatives. Even the policy issues for which he was most widely known as a public advocate initially had been the idea of one staff person or another. For example, one of the issues to which Sargent became most deeply committed, "deinstitutionalization" of individuals in large state facilities, was the inspiration of Kramer and of Human Services Secretary Peter Goldmark. Sargent's own particular stamp on this policy-choosing process was not his emphasis on the substantive development of the policy, but his ability to choose policies that were both politically acceptable and consistent with both his public stance and private values.

The fact that he did not come into office with strong positions was in part the result of the circumstances under which he became governor. As a candidate for lieutenant governor, his job was not to advocate programs or policies but, rather, to make public appearances and to create a generally favorable impression. When he ran for his first full term in 1970, he was already the incumbent and his job was not to develop strong policy stands or make speeches about what government should do but to defend the actions of his administration. Many of his policy positions were inherited from the Volpe administration. This fact, combined with his own stylistic preferences, meant that he did not develop any strong feelings about advocating innovations or programs in any single policy area.

One of the consequences of this style was that the quality of the policy decisions made in his administration depended not only on the wisdom of Sargent's choices among alternatives but also on the importance and nature of the issues that got onto his agenda. Flannery, the chief of staff, though politically conservative was temperamentally very similar to the governor. He seldom expressed strong policy preferences initially, instead serving as a kind of deputy mediator. He described his own shortcoming in working for Sargent as "being too much like him. I'm a good reporter of ideas and controversies. They don't get short-circuited. But I'm not likely to come up with any initiatives that will make him jump out of his chair."[11] This meant that, in effect, Kramer and his staff or one or more of the ten cabinet secretaries bore the burden of formulating proposals for change in policy and of calling them to the governor's attention.

Despite Kramer's quickness and his ability to spot a crisis issue and the consequent need for action on the governor's part, he was not able to keep up with the mass of detail or activities of all the agencies. The burden of this job fell on individual specialists on the policy staffs. The results varied greatly from individual to individual and from agency to agency. Some agencies had no one on the governor's staff monitoring them at all and therefore did not involve the governor in any policy decision unless it was one that individuals in the agency made on their own initiative and chose to raise. Because individual staff members themselves had no staffs and were generally given broad mandates, such as responsibility for "the environment" or "children's services" or "transportation," they had to choose a limited number of issues on which to inform themselves and restrict their attempts to change policy to these areas. Often their success or failure at initiating measures depended on the degree of hostility or good feeling within a given agency toward them personally or toward the governor. Even the most astute and best liked of the staff members who built up goodwill within their agencies were able to take "noncrisis" initiatives on only a limited number of issues. For example, Stephen Weiner, whose field was health and who was among the specialists perhaps the best liked and most respected by his agencies, had to limit his initiatives in the field of health regulation. His own interest and the fact that he is a lawyer by training led him to devote any free time he had to developing proposals for a strong health regulatory agency. Because of the complexity of the field and the governor's own style of making decisions on the basis of proposals, any policy initiative or change made within the state health care bureaucracy was likely to be the result of action by the agencies' own personnel, Weiner's initiative, or a combination of the two.

Maintaining a Position Under Pressure

Just as a governor has to deal with an agency or agencies to change policy, he may also become involved in backing up lower level employees who support or enforce a policy that arouses opposition either within the government itself or outside it. Sargent and his staff were steadfast at providing support for a beleaguered policy or group of individuals within an agency who advocated a position once that position was known. Sargent's forte was making practical policy decisions with which he could live. Because it was his own stylistic preference, he often listened to various views on an issue in oral argument before him. He seldom made a decision on an issue having heard only one side, especially when conflicting views were represented within his own staff. Perhaps his single greatest talent as a politician was his ability to sense how powerful his opposition was on issues, particularly on issues where the opposition was outside the administrative agencies. He enjoyed backing up beleaguered individuals or policies once he had decided that their position was sound. As one Sargent observer put it: "The most fun thing personally for the governor which he did in a long time was to back up Jerry Miller. [Miller was the director of the Department of Youth Services who stirred up an enormous controversy by shutting down all of the state's training schools for juveniles, arguing that they were inhumane and a training ground for further crime.] The more the legislature howled, the stronger the support he gave."[12]

The governor's strong and usually consistent stands on policy positions once he made a decision were reinforced by the basic competence of his staff at gathering facts and their general credibility with the agencies with which they dealt. Although the staff was not always able to take the initiative on a policy, once an issue became "controversial" and was important enough to come to the governor's or his staff's attention, they generally had little difficulty in finding out who was involved in the dispute and in figuring out ways to put the final authority of the governor behind the decision. If two staff members disagreed or if a staff member and an agency head disagreed on a policy or on how to defend it, the system of advocacy and of hearing out both sides of the issue usually went into effect, ending, if necessary, with a decision by the governor himself.

This system was further reinforced by Sargent's own strong feeling that if employees stayed within any broad policy guidelines that he articulated, they should be allowed to behave as they wished and receive his full backing. Perhaps the best example of this was his support of his constantly beleaguered commissioner of public welfare, Steven Minter. Although welfare was an area subject to constant scrutiny and criticism by the public, Sargent backed Minter up publicly on every issue, even when he did not know many of the details of the issues raised.

Setting a Tone, Keeping Morale High

Another important management function that a chief executive handles is that of setting a favorable tone for those who work at all levels of the administration. This may involve his spending time maintaining communications with and conveying a sense of personal interest in individuals or in agencies and providing incentives to employees to perform well. This contact may also be undertaken to engender personal loyalty to the governor among employees who might not have direct contact with him or with his immediate staff. In the long run, the tone of the governor's administration may also be influenced by his willingness to hire professionals, to be thought of as a professional himself, and to take stands on controversial or difficult issues.

Though Sargent was generally firm in his support of employees on controversial issues and set a tone of being a strong governor in time of crisis, he and his staff spent only a limited amount of time touring state facilities or programs. The time he spent with state employees other than his own senior staff members was minimal, and one of the complaints that junior members of his staff had was that they seldom saw him. He was not given to making unscheduled visits to state offices or institutions. The style of his staff reflected Sargent's own style on this. In talking about their jobs, only one of the several dozen staff members mentioned the importance of visiting state facilities and programs and of talking to the employees who work in them. Sargent was a fine campaigner and liked to move around the state for political gatherings, but he made few attempts to campaign for the support of state employees. His office and staff engaged in relatively little writing of letters of commendation or special notices of work well done. The net result was that most state employees drew their image of the governor from the media and from the other vehicles available to the general public, and not from any sort of personal contact with him or with his staff.

The tone-setting function that Sargent took most seriously

was recruiting administrators for professional positions. He hired personnel both from within and outside the state based on their professional competence and reputation. Aided by the fact that the state capital is located in the city of Boston, he attracted scores of job applications from individuals with a great variety of professional skills who could have worked in any number of government jurisdictions. He and his staff were willing to take progressive, innovative stands on such controversial issues as penal reform, reform of the juvenile justice system, and transportation planning. Though his stands on these issues made him unpopular with many of the state's career employees, this characteristic allowed him to attract many young professionals, some of whom took considerable cuts in salary to join him.

Mediating Disputes Among Different Agencies or Factions Within Agencies

As the designated final authority in the administrative hierarchy, a governor must mediate disputes over programs or resources that agencies or individuals are unable to settle by themselves. He may accomplish this by a variety of means including getting agreement by promises of favorable rewards in the future for any or all parties involved; getting an agreement by reminding one or more of the disputants of his help in the past; justifying any decision that he makes in terms of his executive prerogative; or enforcing as far as possible a decision in favor of one side or another, depending on the merits or policy implications of the issue, or, at times, on his favorable disposition toward one of the parties involved.

Because Sargent himself was remote from the day-to-day workings of the state agencies, most of the disputes between agencies fell to Kramer to mediate. Although Kramer enjoyed mixed reviews throughout the government, he was universally respected for his intelligence and his ability to grasp quickly the facts of a situation. More important, he was known to speak for the governor in most instances and to have the governor's strong support. Agencies occasionally appealed a Kramer decision to

Flannery, who in turn decided whether or not it was important enough for the governor himself to make a decision. This was the exception rather than the rule, however, for two reasons. First, Sargent, like many other executives, did not enjoy performing this function, especially when it involved his having to go on record as being in favor of one agency's position and opposed to another's. He preferred to deal with agencies when they brought him good news or when he did not have to use up "credit" that he had built up in one agency to soothe feathers ruffled by a decision that went against it.

Second, disputing agencies knew they could generally expect a fast and reasoned resolution of the dispute from Kramer. Kramer was able to be responsible for his enormous job largely by virtue of his ability to analyze rapidly the facts of a situation, so these arguments tended to be made orally and the decisions often favored the agency that sent the most articulate person to plead its case.

Marketing

Often a governor's management of his administration and the policies that come out of it depend on his ability to "market" or "sell" a political or policy issue within the bureaucracy or to the public at large. This may involve his polishing or packaging a rough or partially developed idea. Or, at times, it may require working on a fully developed policy or set of policies to make them palatable or appealing to people beyond the boundaries of the narrow constituency where they were developed.

Of all the functions of managing the agencies and their policies that Sargent and his staff engaged in, the single one they handled best and enjoyed most was the "marketing" of a policy or of an agency's image, especially when this marketing involved selling something to the public. This was the result of a combination of factors. First, Sargent was an acknowledged master in his use of television for difficult situations involving particularly controversial public policies. In the three conflicts with the legislature during which he faced the most extreme public scrutiny—those involving public welfare, corrections, and transportation—he "took his case to the people" on prime time television, boosted his rating in public opinion polls, and survived the crisis. His ability to "talk to the people" about his problems was a powerful political asset and one on which he frequently relied.

Second, perhaps the greatest collective talent of his staff lay in their liking and talent for public relations and marketing work. Of the senior staff, Flannery, Reardon, and Teichner were all former journalists. Kramer too demonstrated considerable talent for figuring out how to package a program. As one of the cabinet secretaries put it: "They've got a bunch of PR geniuses up there [in the governor's office]. Selling snowballs in Alaska would be a breeze for them."[13]

The focus on marketing was the result not only of the talents and inclinations of the staff and the governor but also of the general style of the governor's office. Because most of the agency issues the governor's office handled were those that surfaced due to a crisis, the need to make a public statement or response was often pressing; and the burden of doing it was assumed not by the agency involved but by the governor's office itself. What caused this to happen involves a certain amount of circular reasoning. On the one hand, the nature of the governor's job involves handling a large number of unexpected political emergencies. These crises demand quick and public response. On the other hand, one could argue that the style of Sargent and his staff was to ignore an issue until it became or could be defined as a crisis and then to treat it as a marketing or public relations problem, something they enjoyed and were good at doing.

Both staff members in the governor's office and agency personnel point out that this talent for and concentration on marketing had important implications for the general tone of agency management. As one staff member put it: "We answered a crisis—but we answered it with a press release. It's a cosmetic approach to administration. There's no follow-through, no holding the agency responsible. As long as a department doesn't get you into trouble publicly, it can do whatever it wants."[14]

Recruiting

Another management function with which any chief executive has to deal is selection and introduction of personnel into the government. This may simply involve filling vacancies or a new position. A governor may also view personnel recruiting and hiring as a vehicle for ensuring that his own preferences are reflected throughout the government. "Management" for a governor may also involve removing those who are disloyal, incompetent, or unsympathetic and replacing them with loyalists who will carry out his orders or with those to whom he can comfortably delegate responsibility for a policy area or department.

Sargent prided himself on his interest in hiring professionally respected, high-level personnel. This was particularly crucial to him because of his own distinterest in involving himself in day-to-day management of agency business. Both he and his staff actively involved themselves in the search for personnel to fill top administrative positions. In fact, the governor's greatest involvement with most agency heads came when they were appointed. After that, unlike many governors who advocate particular policies for their agencies and who involve themselves with the agencies' activities, both Sargent and his staff remained aloof from the personnel they had carefully selected, intervening only when a crisis arose or when an agency head was clearly violating the general policy guidelines laid down by the governor or his staff. Sargent was also reluctant to fire any of his appointees publicly and did so only twice in the six years that he served as governor. More frequently, if his top appointees were not performing satisfactorily, he persuaded them to resign or simply allowed them to stay on to avoid public confrontations over personnel.

In 1972, Sargent appointed Robert Dumont, a former vice-president for personnel of the New England Life Insurance

Company and a career personnel professional, head of the Governor's Office of State Service, traditionally the locus of the state's patronage operation. Unlike his predecessors, whose role was often to fill the jobs under their jurisdiction with campaign workers loyal to the governor or to key legislators, Dumont focused his attention on building a recruitment network capable of finding the best possible people for jobs at all levels. His job was restructured to include assisting agency heads and cabinet secretaries in meeting their personnel needs as much as responding directly and solely to the governor's political needs.

The focus of the governor's office on professional recruitment techniques and on merit appointments was dictated not only by the governor's own personal bias and by his appointment of Dumont, but also by the decrease in the importance of patronage appointments. Sargent had a strong personal antipathy toward appointing "hacks" to high-level professional jobs such as top positions in important agencies or secretariats. The rigid Massachusetts civil service system covers most of the state's permanent jobs and made it extremely difficult for the governor to appoint people to jobs at his own discretion or to fire people who held those jobs. Only about three thousand full-time jobs become vacant each year in Massachusetts; in recent years, due to austerity measures, many of these jobs have not been filled. Of those remaining, Dumont estimated that only about one hundred could be influenced at all by the governor.[15] In addition, Sargent had some control over approximately six hundred summer jobs at the Metropolitan District Commission's swimming facilities and in the Department of Natural Resources. The Sargent administration did not concentrate much energy on using this relatively small number of jobs for patronage. The rationale behind this policy, pointed out by several staff members, was perhaps best summed up by Chief Secretary Flannery: "It's a trick bag for us to try to use patronage. You can't win on it. For every job you give to somebody you turn nine people away—nine campaign workers or at least voters. Also, you have to remember that the kind of jobs we have up for grabs just aren't as attractive to people as they used to be. Who wants a job as a part-time lifeguard or as a full-time janitor? Nobody—especially in a Republican administration."[16] The overall result of the governor's stance on recruiting personnel was that he picked agency heads and high-level appointees carefully and with an eye toward their stature in their professions. He often appointed people from outside the state service and frequently from outside of Massachusetts, irritating many of the long-time state employees who would have liked to have someone from among their own ranks. At the same time, he did not attempt to force agency heads to hire or fire their employees on the basis of their political leanings or their loyalty to Sargent.

Allocating Resources

A final important "management function" that any governor has to perform involves the allocation of resources. One formal power all chief executives share is the power to submit their budgets to the legislature for its approval. A political executive may choose to become deeply involved in the operations and policies of his agencies by actively participating in the budget process and by meeting his own agenda by expanding or cutting funding or staffing for an agency or for a particular program. He may also involve himself only to the extent of giving an agency an overall budget target and letting the agency decide how to allocate it; or he may "manage" by stipulating particular programs, policies, or personnel that he wants eliminated.

Although initiation of the budget and allocation of resources is usually considered one of the governor's strongest weapons for managing his administrative agencies, neither Sargent nor his staff ever became deeply involved in formulating the budget. No one on Sargent's personal staff of forty professionals had anything resembling training or experience in fiscal management. When Sargent was acting governor, he relied on the expertise and budgetary advice of his close friend Commissioner of Administration and Finance Donald Dwight. After Dwight became lieutenant governor, there was no one on Sargent's staff who filled the position of chief fiscal advisor. Although Sargent continually relied on the advice of the commissioner of administration and finance (a position appointed by him), the individuals who held the job during Sargent's tenure were far more independent of Sargent personally and politically than Dwight had been. In addition, Sargent's control over administration and finance was weakened by the strong loyalties and long-term working relationships that had grown up over the years between the career, second-tier personnel in administration and finance and the career staff of the House and Senate Ways and Means committees of the legislature.

Though Sargent had to sign his budget submission and technically was responsible for its content, he held no budget hearings of his own and involved himself very little in the overall budgetary process. He and his staff did participate in some decisions on resources for specific programs or policies, especially if these were issues on which he had taken a public stand; but they demonstrated little interest in the development of the budget during the course of the fiscal year.

This lack of interest or expertise in the subtleties of the budgetary process was not peculiar to Sargent; it permeated the entire staff. Manipulation of the budgets of the various agencies was not a tool of control that most of the staff enjoyed or felt comfortable using. As one senior staff member put it, "When they start that numbers mumbo-jumbo, my mind turns right off."[17] Almost all of the decisions about how much money to allow for programs and divisions of agencies were made on the basis of a detailed series of budget hearings in the agencies, the secretariats, and administration and finance. Policy made in agencies is often contingent on the level of funding decided in these hearings. Despite the importance of the final product of these hearings for the management and control of the agencies, no one from the governor's staff (including the functional specialists) regularly attended them or attempted to influence their outcome. The review of these decisions in the governor's office before the budget was submitted to the legislature was cursory and involved little more than the addition of funding for priority programs and reduction or elimination of funding for others. For the agencies, the result of this procedure was that formulation of much of the budget submission was delegated downward, usually to the secretaries and sometimes, by default, to the agencies themselves. The agency heads did battle with the cabinet secretaries. When they had differences of opinion with specific secretaries, the agency heads sometimes appealed to the secretary of administration and finance. Unlike some other states, where the governor's office is intimately involved with the entire budget-making process and uses it as a means of day-to-day control and influence,[18] in Massachusetts during the Sargent administration the governor and his staff remained aloof from the development of budgetary issues, especially those involving technical or time-consuming details. Sargent and his staff seldom used the budget as a mechanism for controlling the daily operation of the agencies, foregoing one potentially powerful method of persuading agencies to be responsive to the governor.

Many of the individual functions involved in managing the state are not unique to the public sector. The public sector chief executive, however, has no perfect analog in business. There are two important reasons for defining as explicitly as possible what management means for a publicly elected chief executive. First, it puts the issue in the particular context of the governor's world, a complex, public, and highly political environment. Second, it provides some base for comparison among executives. All governors have to deal with the management functions described. All deal with them differently. During the course of their tenure in office individual executives shift the balance of their attention among these functions. Therefore one of the clues to each governor's style is how he balances these functions off against each other, ignoring some, focusing on others, and in so doing arriving at his particular style of managing the state.

Notes

1

Perhaps the best example of an attempt to apply this theory to the government is the report of the Commission on Organization of the Executive Branch of Government, "General Management of the Executive Branch." For excellent critiques of attempts to apply this logic to the public sector, see Harold Seidman's *Politics, Position and Power* and Robert Wood's "The Metropolitan Governor." Seidman sums up this orthodoxy on page 4 of the introduction to his book:

The devils to be exorcised are overlapping and duplication, and confused or broken lines of authority and responsibility. Entry into the Nirvana of Economy and Efficiency can be obtained only by strict adherence to sound principles of executive branch organization. Of these the most essential are the grouping of executive branch agencies as nearly as possible by major purposes so that "by placing related functions cheek-by-jowl the overlaps can be eliminated, and of even greater importance coordinated policies can be developed"; and the establishment of a clear line of command and supervision from the President down through his department heads to every employee with no subordinate possessing authority independent from that of his superior.

2

See, for example, Hugo Uyterhoeven, "General Managers in the Middle," *Harvard Business Review*, March-April 1972; Henry Mintzberg, "The Manager's Job: Folklore and Fact," *Harvard Business Review*, July-August, 1975; Edward Wrapp, "Good Managers Don't Make Policy Decisions," *Harvard Business Review*, September-October, 1967; and Paul Lawrence and Jay Lorsch, "New Management Job: The Integrator," *Harvard Business Review*, November-December, 1967.

3

Kenneth Andrews, *The Concept of Corporate Strategy*, p. 3 ff.

4

Ibid., p. 13.

5

Ibid., p. 37.

6

See Chester Barnard, *The Functions of the Executive* and Philip Selznick, *Leadership in Administration*.

7

Interview with Francis Sargent. Because this interview was "off the record," most descriptions of Sargent's comments will not contain direct quotations but will follow closely his views as he expressed them.

8
Ibid.

9
Interview with Albert Kramer. Unlike several of the other staff members interviewed, Kramer expressed no hesitation at being quoted by name. Although there will be some quotes attributed to specific individuals, many references will identify someone only as a "junior" or a "senior" member of the governor's staff.

10
Although most of any governor's job involves "crisis management," not all governors are as preoccupied with it as Sargent was. When Richard Ogilvie was governor of Illinois, for example, he set up a Bureau of the Budget to formulate long-range management and fiscal objectives. As a member of that staff, I observed that he spent a great deal of time on day-to-day management of the affairs of his agencies, often working far into the night going over individual line item appropriations in his budget submission. Sargent's successor, Michael Dukakis, in the early months of his administration was heavily criticized for behaving in exactly the opposite manner from Sargent and immersing himself so deeply in the details of every issue that he had no sense of perspective on the relative importance of the issues with which he was dealing.

Thus it can be argued that although all chief executives must spend considerable time and energy on publicly perceived crises, there can be variations in the amount and nature of "crisis management" that depend not only on the number of crises that occur but also on the style of the individual chief executive.

11
Interview with Jack Flannery.

12
Interview with Martin Linsky.

13
Interview with Peter Goldmark.

14
Interview with a junior member of the governor's staff who asked not to be named.

15
Interview with Robert Dumont.

16
Interview with Jack Flannery.

17
Ibid.

18
Many governors have incorporated trained fiscal personnel into their own staffs and use them not only to review the budget but also to develop highly sophisticated strategies to control their agencies through fiscal management. For a detailed discussion of this see Allen Schick, *Budget Innovation in the States.*

3
Gubernatorial Style in Managing the State

In the common parlance of politics, the descriptions of chief executives as "managers" and as "leaders of large organizations" often are used interchangeably. In fact they imply quite different things. All governors have to perform certain management functions, but they perform these functions according to their own preferences and styles. Just as it is important to identify what the management functions are that they perform, it is also necessary to understand the dimensions along which they vary in carrying them out and the kinds of choices they make that determine their individual styles of leadership.

Leadership in any large organization is a highly personalized commodity. Implicit in any definition of leadership is some notion of uniqueness of style or attributes that distinguish and identify both the leader and those who are led. Every governor develops his own leadership style. This style does not depend as much on the formal powers that he has or on the number of orders that he gives as it does on how he chooses to spend his time, what resources he uses, and whose advice and pleas for support he heeds.

Understanding the kinds of variation in gubernatorial leadership style is essential to drawing conclusions about the overall effectiveness of a chief executive's management and about how he compares with other chief executives. How he chooses to use his resources in managing agencies and how many of these resources he chooses to devote to management may be a legitimate criterion for judging his performance. In addition, a governor's leadership style may be important in defining the nature of his relationship with agencies. The mesh or clash between his style and the particular style of the agency with which he is dealing may be as important as the substance of policies he espouses in determining his success or failure at controlling the agency's behavior.

This chapter will look at how Sargent's own leadership style and the choices he made affected his management of state government. Sargent's relationship to the agencies was often directly influenced by the obligations he had as governor, by how management issues got on his agenda, and by how he used the resources available to him. By looking at these questions it is possible to understand not only some of the determinants of Sargent's own particular style of management but also some of the dimensions along which all chief executives may vary in their personal leadership styles.

How Do the Other Roles that a Governor Has to Play Affect His Job As Manager?

A governor, even if he wants to, cannot manage all the time. The extent to which he is able to spend time and energy managing his agencies is dependent on the other functions he has to perform and on their importance to him. Perhaps the most significant thing that can be said about Francis Sargent in this respect is that he did not especially enjoy the detailed work of agency management and therefore did not accord it a favored position among his duties. His job as "manager of the bureaucracy" and the demands it imposed on him for his time, attention, and resources had to be balanced against other demands. His own preference to stay clear of the particulars of agency management was reinforced by the fact that his ability to appear a credible manager was heavily dependent on his success at building resources and power in performing his other functions. This was especially true of his ability to remain a successful political figure because his legitimacy as an elected executive depended on his maintaining, or appearing to maintain, electoral support. It is therefore worthwhile to look briefly at the other roles Sargent had to perform and at the importance and attention he accorded them.

An analysis of Sargent's calender indicates that he spent well over half of his time performing what generally might be labeled the "ceremonial" functions of the governor.[1] These include proclamation signings, swearing-in of public officials, and, especially, large numbers of public appearances. Appearances at ceremonial occasions are intimately tied to any ongoing campaigning a governor does and are often his best way of staying in the public eye. In Sargent's case, the jobs of ceremonial head of government and of campaigner were especially tightly linked and took large amounts of his time. There were two primary reasons for this. First, he was an ebullient and skilled campaigner who enjoyed public appearances. Unlike many governors who neither relish the role of ceremonial head of the government nor perform it with polish, Sargent thrived on it. In addition, to a large extent the Sargent political organization revolved around him personally. Although he is a Republican, Sargent's relationship with the state Republican party was strained to the point of involving Sargent in public disputes with the Massachusetts party leadership. The Republican state committee regarded him with suspicion because of his liberal policies, his appointment of many Democrats to positions in his administration, his refusal to back unilaterally all party candidates, and his lukewarm response to the candidacy of Richard Nixon and Spiro Agnew. Sargent, in turn, did not rely heavily on the state Republican party organization but instead built "Governor Sargent Committees" in each county in the state. Although several times he attempted to purge the Republican State Committee of his opponents, he relied on his own organization to attract the Independents and Democrats whom he needed to survive in Massachusetts, where a large majority of registered voters are Democrats and Independents. His organization was personally based, so public appearances were extremely important to his money-raising and general campaign efforts. Responding to these combined duties as ceremonial head of state, candidate, and head of his own electoral organization not only was more pleasant personally for him than spending time managing the agencies but also kept him out of his office and used up one of his most valuable resources, his own time.

Sargent's role as spokesman to other branches and levels of government did not greatly interest him or his staff, and consequently they devoted little time to it. Although any governor must deal with the legislature, for several reasons Sargent did not mobilize an especially effective or lively effort to do this. First, during the six years Sargent was governor the General Court of Massachusetts was overwhelmingly Democratic, and partisan resistance to Sargent programs and initiatives was steady. In addition even the Republican minority had no strong loyalty to Sargent as party leader and often balked at his initiatives. His chances of being able to work closely with such a legislature and at the same time appear to be a forceful executive were low. Instead, Sargent's strategy was often to avoid the costs of dealing with the General Court and to portray himself and his policies as the "victims" of a partisan and parochial legislature.

In addition to the fact that the setting for dealing with the legislature was not favorable to Sargent, he did not devote an enormous amount of time to it because his staff was neither especially interested in it nor especially talented at dealing with it. His legislative liaison was a pleasant and mild ex-legislator who had limited interest in or taste for lobbying and arm-twisting bills through the legislature. Sargent's staff kept no records of favors they had done for particular legislators and they made few attempts to change votes or to lobby on any issues except those that seemed within their grasp.

The governor's unwillingness to deal with the legislature can also be explained by the fact that neither the governor nor his staff members showed any particular fondness or respect for the legislature as an institution. Sargent had not served as a legislator. Two of his staff members (Kramer and Morrow) were former representatives, but when members of the governor's staff dealt with the legislature, they characteristically did so with a good deal of arrogance and in a manner that indicated they felt they were dealing from a superior position.[2] This combination of overwhelming partisan opposition and lack of staff interest and skill at dealing with the legislature meant that Sargent did not devote much time or energy to it. The importance of legislative support or opposition to agency budgets and policies also affected Sargent's ability to influence the outcomes of individual agencies' interactions and dealings with the legislature. This was true both in his enforcing his own policy preferences and in his preventing agency personnel from dealing directly with the legislature and paying little attention to him.

Sargent also took only a limited number of initiatives in dealing and cooperating with the state's other constitutional officers. Perhaps the main reason for this was that during the six years he was in office the other constitutional officers were Democrats. The job of attorney general has always been one potential stepping stone to the governor's office in Massachusetts. Sargent chose to ignore the attorney general as much as possible rather than to attempt to bargain or to joust with him over issues of concern to both of them. Attorney General Robert Quinn was not nearly so aloof from Sargent. He ran for governor in the Democratic primary in 1974, emphasizing in his campaign his investigations of the legality of many actions of Sargent's agencies.

Sargent did not devote much of his own time to dealing with other government jurisdictions, and he did not organize his staff so that the job fell naturally to any one of them. He had a representative in Washington who attempted to keep track of the Massachusetts congressional delegation and to serve as a liaison to large federal agencies, but his ties to the Nixon administration were neither strong nor close. As the Republican governor of the only state in the union in which Richard Nixon did not receive a majority of the popular vote cast in the 1972 election, he was not in a good bargaining position with the Nixon administration. He exacerbated his isolation from the national administration by being a spokesman for the liberal wings of the New England and national Republican governor's organizations, particularly on such issues as welfare, corrections, and the environment. In addition, he did not hold a prominent place in the hierarchy of the national Republican party. This meant that the little time he spent dealing with the federal government was as an advocate for a specific cause or as a supplicant, begging for funds. The consequences of this for his management of the agencies were twofold. First, he had no easy or special access to federal monies to supplement state appropriations. Second, many of the agencies that built up special relationships with their federal counterparts did it without his help and therefore had access to funding and expertise that allowed them independence from him.

Sargent had no formal ongoing relationship or channel of communications with the cities and towns of Massachusetts, including Boston. Robert Wood argued in 1949 that the City of Boston and its problems are so influential for any governor of Massachusetts that "the organization of the executive branch is best discussed in terms of aids or deterrents to the governor's representation of the Boston interest."[3] The major movement of population to suburbs outside the Boston city limits made this not as true during the Sargent administration as it had been in 1949. But because of the overlap of government services as well as the location of the electorate in the state, cities in general and Boston in particular were important to Sargent. Despite this fact, however, neither the governor nor any staff person attempted to keep track of Boston's activities on a day-to-day basis or to work on a series of joint programs or policy plans. Kevin White, the mayor of Boston, had been Sargent's opponent in the 1970 gubernatorial campaign. Sargent kept himself informed of White's activities to the extent that they made him a potential rival and cooperated with him on issues on which both men could gain. However, neither in Sargent's own office nor in his administrative agencies was there a formalized liaison to the City of Boston. Kramer left his job as urban affairs advisor to become chief of the policy staff, and his old job was never filled. The major crises involving the City of Boston and other muncipalities were handled on an issue-by-issue basis through informal channels of negotiation.

Sargent, like most other chief executives, devoted enormous amounts of time and personal resources to the duties of a governor that traditionally would not be regarded as "management." Most of his attention had to be directed to one primary objective: ensuring his political survival. Even when he "managed," he often did so because handling a crisis involving the agencies was important to his political future. Much of his ability to manage the agencies depended on his success at being able to perform these other roles credibly and to build up his resources with other institutions of government and with the electorate. These resources useful in managing the agencies could have been built up in a variety of different places with different results. Sargent's choice of investing his time primarily in his electoral organization, in campaigning, and in public appearances was the result both of his need to preserve his political constituency and of his own personal style.

For Sargent, the job of performing the managerial functions commonly associated with running a large organization often had to be forgone in favor of more pressing matters. If they were done at all, they had to be carried out by staff members or administrators in line agencies acting in behalf of the governor. The irony of this kind of management is that precisely because a political executive draws his legitimacy from being the single person elected to fill the job of governor, his managerial authority is difficult to delegate. Though Sargent supported his chief staff personnel in their policy decisions, there were many management issues on which he was legally and formally the final authority. Even if disputes were resolved or policies handled by virtue of his having delegated them to a staff member, he was often viewed as a weak executive by his agency personnel precisely because it was known that he had not made the final decision himself.

How Does a Management Issue Get on the Governor's Agenda?

One important dimension along which governors differ is the

importance they accord obligations other than management and the capital or leverage their performance of these obligations gives them in the political and administrative system. Equally important in understanding how chief executives manage and how they differ from each other is the question of how issues involving agencies get on their agendas in the first place. There is great variation among executives on this point. The way an issue gets on the governor's agenda and the extent to which a governor can control it may vary because of the differences in states. For example, one might speculate that a governor of a heavily populated, highly industrial state like Massachusetts or New York might have to spend more time dealing with issues put on his agenda by well-organized constituencies than the governor of a state like Wyoming or Idaho, where the population is less dense and where crises are likely to occur less frequently. In addition, how issues get on a chief executive's agenda may vary because of the style and interests of the person who holds the office. For example, in this respect Francis Sargent was extremely different from Richard Ogilvie of Illinois. Though both Sargent and Ogilvie were Republican governors of large industrial states, their agendas often consisted of very different kinds of issues. Ogilvie was fascinated by the question of how well the bureaucracy was working. He spent a great deal of time trying to measure the efficiency and effectiveness of agencies and working to improve the performance of large organizations he felt were not doing well. Sargent, on the other hand, when given a choice rarely put this kind of issue on the top of his agenda and, in fact, actively avoided working on questions of this kind as much as possible. Differences of this kind may indicate a good deal both about a particular governor's personal commitment and style and about the reasons for the autonomy or control with which individual agencies operate.

There are three distinctly different ways in which an issue can get on a chief executive's agenda. The first involves issues put on the agenda by the governor himself. A governor may take a firm stand on an issue or set of issues that he wants implemented, changed, or handled in the agencies because of his own personal commitment to them. The hallmark of the group of governors who might be labeled "activists" is the large number of these kinds of issues they publicly place on their agencies. This may involve overseeing a single set of issues during a limited period of time or it may involve a governor's "adoption" of a policy area or agency that becomes his pet project throughout his administration. In either case, he becomes closely identified with the management of this particular issue or agency because he has chosen it, because he has taken a strong stand on which his position is known from the outset, and because his own credibility is tied up with how it fares.

The second way a management issue may get onto the governor's agenda is if the public or some large group of the electorate puts it there. This kind of issue is similar in many ways to the first kind. Though the chief executive may not have been deeply involved with a particular department or agency, he must take a strong stand on the issue immediately because the electorate as a whole or some important segment of it may *see* him as responsible.[4] As on the first kind of issue, he becomes personally involved at the outset and his ability, real or perceived, to deal with the agencies involved and to convince or coerce them to respond to him becomes crucial. These are often "crisis" situations, such as a prison revolt or discovery of major fraud or errors in a welfare department. In instances of this sort, where his own credibility is at stake, his role as manager of the agencies may take on overwhelming importance and may force him to become intimately involved with the agencies. Even if one single issue is not important enough to determine his electoral future, the cumulative "box score" of how many issues with which he was closely identified he won or lost may become extremely important.

The third distinct kind of management issue that may get on the governor's agenda is different from the first two because of its visibility, its implications, and the demands that are made on the governor. These issues could be labeled "technocratic" or "bureaucratic" issues and are characterized by the fact that they first surface within the administrative agencies or because of a highly technical problem with which the agencies deal.[5] They may be the result of a clash between agencies over jurisdiction, method of operation, or allocation of scarce resources. They may involve highly technical issues that because of their complexity or because of the expertise required to understand them have little potential for arousing immediate public concern or public pressure. At least in its initial stage, this kind of issue may work its way up the administrative hierarchy to be dealt with by agency heads, commissioners, or division directors. Though the issue may become publicly visible, the individuals held responsible by those following the situation are likely to be administrators identified with one particular agency or substantive area of the bureaucracy. For example, a commissioner of public health may be perceived as the immediately responsible official in a controversy over whether a hospital should be allowed to expand. The first contact the governor's office has with such an issue is through a staff person. If the issue cannot be resolved, it may work its way up to the governor for a decision. Unlike issues on which he is personally involved, however, in this situation his major role is as mediator, not as advocate. His job is to be above the fray, to listen to arguments made by both staff and line personnel, and to hand down a decision. Although he may eventually end up with credit for such a policy or program, he does not involve himself initially either by visibly taking a strong stand or by going to war with or exerting strong pressure on the agency or agencies involved. In this situation, unlike those in which the governor is involved from the beginning, the advocates tend to be agency or staff personnel and it is their credibility, not the governor's, that is tied up with resolving or winning the issue.[6]

Technocratic issues are not immediately public, but a chief executive may sustain "losses" on them that may affect his ability to manage. He may become known for taking no initiatives at all on technical issues or for having an incompetent group of people working for him. Or he may "lose" because by deciding in favor of one advocate or another he may destroy the morale, effectiveness, or goodwill of a staff person or agency head who in day-to-day activities is supposed to speak for him. It is also possible to find out a good deal about the nature of the long-term strength and responsiveness of the relationship between the governor and any particular set of agencies by looking at whether the governor attempts to manage and maintain an interest in an agency only at a time when his personal credibility is at stake or whether he takes a more active interest in the day-to-day workings and activities of the agency.

Though it is possible to find individual examples of all three kinds of issues' getting onto Sargent's agenda, it is clear that his own style and personal preferences dictated that most of the time he spent on management issues involved those he dealt with because he perceived a public demand that he manage or avert a crisis. When Sargent took office, he had no strong personal commitments to particular agency policies. His natural inclination was toward being a mediator rather than an activist, and this personal preference caused him to wait for technocratic issues to surface on their own rather than to rummage around the bureaucracy searching them out. Because his own and his staff's temperamental preferences were to deal with crisis issues, often resulting in the "crisis of the day" receiving enormous amounts of attention, most of Sargent's management effort was directed toward dealing with a few highly visible issues. The kinds of bureaucratic issues that had little potential for ballooning to crisis proportions often went unnoticed. Whether there was any initiative taken on them at all depended heavily on the strength and imagination of the staff person assigned responsibility for that functional area, of the cabinet secretary, or of agency personnel.

Policy areas in which the Sargent administration became known for taking initiatives included health regulation, environmental policy, provision of children's services, right to privacy legislation, transportation policy, "deinstitutionalization," wel-

fare management, and correctional reform. Sargent took firm
stands on environmental management, correctional reform, and
deinstitutionalization after specific possibilities for policy in
these areas were presented to him by his staff. He associated
himself closely with bold policies in these areas and had to take
an ongoing interest in the agencies that dealt with them. When
he had to fire his radical and highly controversial commissioner
of corrections, John Boone, public response focused on the governor personally and on his ability to handle the situation. The
issue became a crisis as well as a question of personal commitment for the governor and caused him to become intimately involved with the Department of Corrections.

The governor's initiatives in welfare made him equally visible
and vulnerable. Like his concern over correctional issues, Sargent's interest in managing the welfare issue was the result not
of a strong set of beliefs about welfare management but of the
chronic sense of public dismay about the Department of Public
Welfare. Sargent asked that the state assume control of the welfare system and made major administrative changes in department operations because of the system's high cost and because
of the public's anger over the issue. He as governor was seen as
responsible for the welfare issue, so he *had* to take initiative and
had to familiarize himself with the department and with the
most controversial of its policies.

Sargent's moratorium on highway building was not as clear
cut a response to crisis, but it was a response to crisis just the
same. His announcement of the highway moratorium was pre-
cipitated both by public outcry and by his having been persuaded by Kramer and a series of allies from a variety of antihighway constituencies that the issue had reached crisis proportions.[7]

On all of these issues involving an immediate and highly visible position taken by the governor, control of the agencies involved became an important issue for the governor and his staff.
These agencies were often closely scrutinized and constantly
had broad (and sometimes strict) parameters of action laid

down for them by someone close to the governor, if not by the governor himself. Their performance was closely watched, and commissioners or high-ranking agency personnel were removed from office or resigned at a far greater rate than those of other agencies.[8]

Some of the policy positions for which Sargent was known did *not* involve immediate action on his part initially but instead surfaced first at lower levels of the government. These included protection of the public from large-scale data gathering by government and limitation of access to data-gathering facilities, creation of an Office for Children to extend the state's network of children's services, and initiation of a strong health regulatory mechanism. These issues differed markedly from the crisis issues both in the governor's treatment of them and in the consequences of that treatment for the state's agencies. They involved problems that normally would have been considered "technicalities" of running a bureaucracy and as such might have escaped public notice indefinitely. They usually surfaced because of the particular preferences, interests, and talents of someone in an agency or a junior "functional specialist" on the governor's staff or a combination of both. For example, the emphasis on children's services (particularly on foster care and adoption) came from Elton Klebanoff, a lawyer who by adopting a child had become involved with the state's array of children's service agencies. Andrew Klein, who initiated the effort to block massive accumulation of data on individuals by the state and federal governments, had picked the issue as a nonthreatening one with which to deal with the agencies for which he had been designated the governor's liaison and in order to focus his job beyond the amorphous assignment of being a special assistant for welfare, law enforcement, and public safety.

The staff member from the governor's office worked closely with agency personnel on each of these issues, providing support for and receiving support from the agency involved. Both Klebanoff and Stephen Weiner, the staff person most responsible for initiating the state's health regulatory legislation, made an effort to spend much time in the agencies assigned to them and based their opinions of what should be done more on the views of the personnel working in the agencies than on the guidance of the senior staff in the governor's office. The circumstances under which Weiner secured cooperation within the Executive Office of Human Services and the Department of Public Health were among the most fortuitous of any experienced by any functional specialist on the governor's staff. He knew the agencies and personnel involved in health regulation well and enjoyed the goodwill and confidence of the agency staffs. He began to work for the state at the same time that the secretariat's leading expert on health did, and he helped recruit and hire the commissioner of public health. He showed himself to be willing to work on the details of health regulatory policy and functioned at times as if he were a staff member of the agency. Finally, he enjoyed the confidence of both Kramer and the governor and was known in the governor's office as a person who asked for attention only when it was absolutely necessary.

The crisis orientation of Sargent's style was not without its costs, particularly as it affected the relationship between the governor and his agencies. There was intense competition among staff members and between staff members and agency personnel to provide a solution in a crisis. Because Sargent liked to hear all sides of an issue and then decide it, there tended to be losers and winners. Agency heads and agency personnel resented getting attention from the governor's office only in times of crisis, when they were often at their most disorganized. This style also promoted competition for the governor's time between the staff and the secretariats and agencies. The staff was concerned with and liked "managing crisis," even if the issue involved was simply the "crisis of the day." The agency and secretariat personnel, on the other hand, did not tend to see the major issues that concerned them as potential electoral crises for the governor but, rather, as issues that affected their working conditions and the capacity of the agencies to deal with policy. Finally, although there were some unspectacular policy initiatives on which agency personnel worked closely with members of the governor's staff, there was a certain randomness about these. They were highly dependent on whether anyone on the governor's staff was assigned to their agency and on the personality, talent, and personal preferences of the governor's staff member who was assigned.

What Management Resources Does a Governor Have?

Having looked at variations in executive agendas, it is important to ask, once an item gets on a governor's agenda, what influences how it is managed and the success or failure of an executive's intervention? A governor's ability to manage a particular incident or to control an agency over a sustained period of time depends, more than on anything else, on the resources he is able to mobilize. Resources vary in kind and in importance. A resource is any identifiable set of goods, services, or skills that help someone reach a desired end. Political resources may be useful in only one situation or may be used continuously over a period of time. Political resources are often highly personalized—a resource for one political executive may not necessarily be a resource for another. For purposes of analysis, political resources important in management may be divided into three categories: personal resources, situational resources, and enabling resources.

Personal Resources

Personal resources include personal traits such as intelligence, humor, verbal facility, and personal political skill. They are the resources most difficult to generalize about because they are highly dependent on the individual manager's particular personality. Richard Neustadt has argued that the most important power a chief executive has is "the power to persuade," describing the chief executive's main task as "to induce them [those agencies with which he is dealing] to believe that what he wants of them is what their own appraisal of their own responsibilities requires them to do in their interest, not his."[9] One could argue that it is in exercising this "power to persuade" that personal resources are especially important, though difficult to identify or catalog from one situation to the next.

Sargent's personal appeal was considerable. Though he was not overwhelmingly articulate, even his detractors conceded that Sargent's charm and humor were among his strongest political assets. He was especially effective at using the media both in campaigns and during crises in his administration because of his ability to project a likeable, easy-going quality. For example, in his debates in 1970 with his Democratic rival for governor, Kevin White, the general consensus of the press was that though White had made his arguments more sharply and more articulately, Sargent had "won" the debates by appearing to be the nicer, more easy-going, less "political" of the two. The fact that he was not an "arm-twister" had both negative and positive implications for his ability to manage. He did not like "horsetrading" and bargaining with political favors, which meant that he did not exercise as much leverage with the legislature, other jurisdictions, his party, and even his own agencies as he might have. On the other hand, he was not negatively perceived as a "politician" who would sell his soul for a vote by either the other branches of the government or by the electorate in general.

Situational Resources

"Situational resources" are those highly diverse sources of help in managing particular situations that vary according to the particular combination of circumstances of an agency and the issues with which it deals. They are not constant in their value. For example, having a close and well-informed relationship with the chairman of the Committee on Ways and Means may be an extremely valuable resource for a governor when he wants to prevent cuts in the state's welfare budget, but it may not necessarily be a resource to him in attempting to pass a measure to change the process of judicial selection. Of all the kinds of resources a governor uses, situational resources are the most variable in their applicability and importance within any single administration. There are four especially salient kinds of situational resources: knowledge of the jurisdiction and of the political climate, technical expertise, clear authority, and the ability to define the management task or objective clearly. In dealing with one agency or situation he is trying to control, a governor may have to rely on his ability to manipulate and master only one of these resources; but in dealing with another situation, he may need to summon several or all of them.

Knowledge of the Jurisdiction and of the Political Climate   One resource that is important to any public manager, especially to a governor, is a detailed knowledge of the particular political environment in which he operates. For a governor whose jurisdiction is broad, this may involve detailed knowledge of the personalites and particular quirks of the other governmental institutions with which he has to deal. It also involves having enough experience to be able to identify key actors in any given political situation and to understand the composition and size of the pool of those politically talented or active in a given area. This kind of knowledge may be particularly important in making management decisions on issues with a long or controversial history or in selecting personnel for new jobs or to fill vacancies.

Sargent, like most governors, had spent most of his life in his native state, Massachusetts. Unlike many other governors, however, his career in Massachusetts government had been confined to jobs in the state bureaucracy in natural resources and public works and did not include service in the legislature, in any other consitutional offices, or in local government. He was familiar with the workings of two state agencies but not with the agencies of administrative oversight like the Exeeutive Office of Administration and Finance. Although as governor he had to deal with a variety of governmental institutions, his only "apprenticeship" had been in an administrative agency. The result of this was that his knowledge of the important actors and of relevant information about the political process was largely confined to the general political climate of Massachusetts and did not include in-depth familiarity with or fondness for such institutions as the legislature or the lower levels of the bureaucracy.

Technical Expertise Another crucial resource in any managerial situation may be technical expertise. Understanding a particular situation fully may require knowledge of one technical area. This may be especially crucial to a public manager at a level below that of the governor because the governor's responsibility is so broad that he could not possibly be an expert in all substantive areas falling under his jurisdiction. Even for a governor, however, technical expertise, or access to someone possessing that expertise who is also loyal to him, may be a crucial management resource. The resource of technical expertise may also involve knowledge of how highly complex general government functions such as personnel systems or resource allocation mechanisms work. It may include an understanding of certain techniques for operations research, capital budgeting, or accounting. On questions that are so highly technical that how the question is put and what choices are outlined may determine the answer, trusted technical expertise may be a crucial management resource.

Sargent was an architect by training and, except in the fields of natural resources and engineering, he had had no formal academic or management training in any of the highly technical fields for which he was responsible. Because he took great pains to recruit competent professionals for high-level government jobs, his access to trusted technical expertise in such areas as transportation, housing, and welfare was good. His own grasp of the details of these particular areas or of the general complexities of administrative management such as budgeting or financial transactions was limited. His style of management was not to be a "details man." This meant that his access to the resources of technical expertise was not based on his own understanding of many issues, that it was highly dependent on the ability of his own appointees in those areas, and that it was extremely variable from one functional area to another.

Clear Authority A third kind of situational resource is presence of clear authority. This authority may stem from the formal legal authority granted by the constitution or by law. It may also be informal and may be the result of a chief executive's ability to convince everyone that he is and should be in control of a situation or an agency. For an elected public manager such as the governor, this authority may come from an electoral victory widely interpreted as a "sweeping mandate." It may also come from the appearance of general support within agencies. In any case, the resource consists of being able to assume control of a situation in a context in which everyone involved believes that the governor has the legitimate right to do so.

The Massachusetts governor's formal authority is broad compared with that of governors in many other states.[10] The governor has a four-year term, can submit his own budget to the legislature, and can hire and fire his cabinet and most commissioners at will. Although Sargent submitted a budget to the legislature each year, he did not have the staff, the expertise, or the personal inclination to develop his budgetary power to be a significant resource and to use it as a mechanism to maintain day-to-day control over his agencies. He was less reluctant to use the power to hire and fire and to make it clear that he had the authority to do this.

Sargent was less adept at establishing his authority where there was no formal grant of power than he was at exercising his constitutional authority. Although he occasionally made policy by use of administrative fiat, he seldom used his budgetary power as a carrot or a stick in asserting his authority over the agencies. Similarly, he made little effort to use his legal staff to interpret agency statutes or regulations to give him leverage with the agencies. Finally, although he did often appeal directly to the electorate for support, very seldom did he use the argument that his decision should be final because of his popular mandate to govern.

Ability to Define the Management Task Clearly A fourth situational resource that may be the most crucial in determining how well an executive is able to manage a problem is his ability to define the job to be accomplished in such a way that it is capable of being reduced to a clear, simple, straightforward task. Whether this resource is present or absent may depend on the governor's ability to reduce a highly complex management situation to be a single task or to define the task in such a way that this becomes possible. It may also depend on the nature of the task itself, which may be so complex that it cannot be simplified without being distorted out of proportion.

Because it varies so much from situation to situation and from agency to agency, it is difficult to generalize about Sargent's use of this resource during his administration. To define the task of the Division of Employment Security ("to mail out unemployment checks") is less difficult than to define the task of the Department of Public Welfare. However, it is true that Sargent's temperament and style did not lead him to want to set fixed goals, especially arbitrary ones, for agencies. He did not deal frequently enough or closely enough with the agencies so that he could constantly measure or evaluate their performance according to any definition of their tasks. This meant that he did not make the effort to state or to simplify the complex goals of most agencies and then to take credit or blame for their performances or failures based on those goals. This was especially true of those agencies whose tasks were difficult to define. Sargent was more likely to ignore these agencies than to insist that they meet any goals set by him.

Enabling Resources

A third set of resources on which any governor draws might be called "enabling resources." These resources are much less likely to vary within any executive's term of office than situational resources and often allow a governor to develop his situational resources. Perhaps the most important of these enabling resources is staff assistance.[11] Also included among these resources are funding for the governor's office, time, and easy access to information. Although these resources are not always separable from situational resources, what distinguishes them from other kinds of resources is that they are not as valuable in and of themselves as they are for *enabling* a governor to build up other kinds of resources. For example, a large and well-funded staff may not by virtue of its existence be valuable to a chief executive but may only become important when it is used to build up other resources. Like all political resources, enabling resources have no inherent value, and their importance depends on whether and how they are used.

Sargent was aided in developing some of the resources necessary to control the agencies by several factors. Compared with many other governors, he had a large, well-financed staff.[12] Perhaps the greatest single determinant of how he was or was not able to utilize resources to manage was the way he designed his staff, which in turn often determined the other resources to which he had the best access. Sargent recognized his own penchant for being a mediator and built into his staff a variety of political views. By ensuring representation of a variety of views along the political spectrum, he made it possible for agencies with extremely diverse interests and for groups outside the government to find allies on his staff. He had some functional policy specialists on his staff who were willing to work as closely with the agencies with which they dealt as with their peers in the governor's office and who knew a great deal about the resources and information necessary to make the agencies behave as they wished. In addition, Sargent received a special bonus by being able to appoint all ten of the first cabinet secretaries to take office. The secretaries were to be "deputy-governors," appointed by the governor to manage clusters of agencies in particular functional areas. By deciding what individuals he was going to appoint, he was able to shape the expectations of both the agencies and the public of what the job of secretary should be and at the same time command personal loyalty from the individuals who took the jobs because they were *his* appointees.

Although the way he constructed his staff and the style with which it operated provided him with access to one set of resources, it also had its costs. The fact that he and his staff opted to concentrate most of their scarce resource of time on maintaining and polishing the governor's electoral image and on managing crises, coupled with the size of the job of running state agencies with a budget of more than $2.5 billion, meant that his attempts at dealing with complicated day-to-day issues were uneven. Particularly because he himself did not devote personal attention to agency matters, his "control" of the administration often depended on the agility with which his staff was able to perform in the difficult "minister-without-portfolio" role. They often had to speak "for the governor" in situations about which the governor, and often the staff member, knew nothing. This difficult role was especially complicated in the Sargent administration for two reasons. First, the incentives for any staff member to want to devote his time to dealing with the big issues, the "crises," were powerful because those issues were high on Sargent's own agenda. But the greater the competition to propose the solution to a crisis, and the more extremely and visibly a staff member stated his own position, the less likely he was to be seen as "speaking for the governor" by the agencies, especially if his solutions "lost" frequently. Second, not only did Sargent create a large number of situations for ministers-without-portfolio, but he also filled these positions, particularly those of "functional specialists," with young inexperienced generalists. An agency that wished to be intractable could mask what it was doing with technicalities and complexities totally unfamiliar to the staff person with responsibility. Also, because few of the members of the governor's staff aspired to holding down their positions after the governor was gone, the agency personnel could count on simply outliving the generalists.

The secretaries and commissioners were appointed by the governor, but because of the Sargent style of operating they were often pitted in deadly competition with the governor's own staff. The staff, busy with dealing with the issue of the day, had little time to focus on any but the most spectacular problems arising in the agencies. The secretaries and commissioners, on the other hand, were hired as full-time administrators and generally concerned themselves with issues different from those with which the staff dealt. Though to a certain extent this meant that responsibility was divided and delegated, it led to bloody battles and extreme competition between the staff and the agencies when each had to compete for the governor's time and attention or when the issue on which the governor had to focus lay in the agencies themselves. Often this competition, coupled with the governor's own reluctance to deal with the legislature, led some agency personnel to negotiate directly with members of the legislature, end-running the governor.

The style and quality of gubernatorial leadership of public agencies varies from governor to governor along several dimensions including the personal temperament of the chief executive, the kind of management he is called on to do, and the resources he can mobilize. But even within one administration, gubernatorial leadership and control can vary greatly from one agency to another. A governor's control and an agency's responsiveness depend not only on conscious decisions on the part of the governor but also on the nature of individual agencies. Different kinds of agencies demand different kinds of management. It is useful briefly to differentiate among kinds of agencies according to the kinds of circumstances in which a governor may deal with them.

The typology of these agencies corresponds roughly to that used to describe how particular issues get on a governor's agenda. Certain agencies require constant scrutiny because the public perceives the issues with which they deal to be on the governor's agenda. Other agencies require constant scrutiny because the governor has dictated that the issues with which they deal be given priority. A third kind of agency receives a governor's attention only when it is responsible for a crisis issue. Finally, some agencies handle matters that seldom if ever get on the governor's agenda.

Those Agencies Requiring Constant Scrutiny

The agencies that demand constant scrutiny may vary from one state to another and from one governor to another, depending on the governor's priorities and his own personal style. These agencies are of two kinds. The first kind is one in which a crisis would be so spectacular or in which the cost of a malfunction would be so high that the governor under no circumstances could afford not to attempt to anticipate it. In Massachusetts, for example, despite the limitations under which he operated in dealing with the bureaucracy, Sargent had to be familiar with the Department of Public Welfare and the Department of Corrections.

The second kind of agency a chief executive must constantly watch differs subtly but significantly from the first kind. It is an agency that must be monitored because it involves such heavy commitment of state money or personnel or such well-organized interests that a problem can cause an outcry or a response from some important constituency or constituencies and, potentially, from the public as a whole. The response to an error or a crisis may not be as clearly immediate as that to the volatile first category, but it may be equally important, either because of the implications for the long-run service provided or because of the importance of the constitutencies involved. In Massachusetts one might cite the Department of Public Works or the Department of Public Health as examples of this second sort of agency. It is also important to point out that for these agencies in Massachusetts the more imminent the threat of crisis, the more likely it is that they will get the kind of attention that the agencies threatening constant spectacular crisis receive.

Those Agencies That Receive Constant Scrutiny Because of the Personal Preferences of the Governor

Some agencies receive attention not because of their size or importance or because they bristle with political bombshells but because the governor has some other interest in them. They may represent a substantive policy area in which he is interested or they may offer a particular resource on which he can capitalize, such as patronage jobs.

Francis Sargent came into office with no strong interest in how any one substantive area or agency of government ran. He was more interested in dealing with agencies on the basis of the seriousness of issues raised within their boundaries than in consistently following any agency or group of agencies that dealt with a substantive policy area of personal interest to him. Perhaps the closest he came to this sort of personal interest was his emphasis on the deinstitutionalization of persons in state facilities. However, he was not a governor like Paul Dever, a Massachusetts chief executive who during his term adopted mental health as his pet issue and chose to keep close track of the Department of Mental Health.

Those Agencies That Receive Gubernatorial Attention Because of a Single Crisis

Every governor has a series of agencies that he generally ignores but that may suddenly become very important because of an unanticipated crisis. For example, in Massachusetts, until the time of the controversy over whether or not to develop the large section of downtown Boston known as Park Plaza, the governor and his staff had no idea who worked in the Department of Community Affairs or what went on there. As a consequence, during the crisis they had to act quickly on the basis of very little previous knowledge of how the agency worked or who in the agency could handle some of the decisions that had to be made. The fact that an agency is the source of a crisis does not necessarily ensure that it can be "crisis-managed," especially if neither the governor nor his staff has invested any resources in it before.

Those Agencies the Governor Leaves Alone

Finally, there is always a series of agencies that a governor makes no effort to control and that he deals with in a limited way or ignores. These agencies fall into two categories: those he leaves alone because of some calculated consideration on his part and those he leaves alone because of the nature of the agencies themselves.

There are several reasons a governor may make a deliberate choice to ignore an agency. First, he may not attempt to exert control over an agency because it performs as he would like. He does not have to use his scarce resources to persuade its personnel to behave as he would like or to make policies he wants because the agency personnel share the chief executive's goals for the agency. During the Sargent administration, the Massachusetts Housing Finance Agency was an example of this kind of agency.

A governor also may not intervene because he realizes that he does not have the resources or the authority to control an agency and may therefore be unwilling to go to battle with it and lose. Even in what may normally be regarded as a crisis, he may hold back from dealing with the issue (as Sargent did, for example, on issues involving higher education in Massachusetts) because he may not be certain of appearing to "win." Or a governor may not deal with an agency because he wants it to be known publicly that he is not fully responsible or in control of that agency. For example, Sargent often made it known that he did not go to battle with the Massachusetts Port Authority because he had no legal control over it.

Finally, a governor may not deal with an agency at all purely because of the nature of the agency. The governor or his staff may see it as having no potential for crisis. For example, in Massachusetts, most governors have assumed that the Massachusetts Department of Agriculture is an agency of this type. An agency may also be left alone because of the highly technical nature of its work. Or it may be ignored because it serves easily identifiable, single, specialized goals. In Massachusetts during the Sargent administration the job of the Division of Employment Security was to send out checks for unemployment compensation, a procedure that varied little from one month to the next.

This chapter has looked at gubernatorial leadership and style and at the characteristics of and limitation on it that affect how the governor manages his agencies and holds them accountable. It has also examined the variation in the kinds of response a governor may make to these agencies and has attempted to explain some general reasons for this variation.

With this as preface, the next chapters will look in depth at several Massachusetts agencies that differ from each other in extent of gubernatorial control and sources of autonomy. The crucial questions with which these chapters deal are how accountable is the agency to the governor, why does he involve himself with or ignore that agency, and what determines the nature of the job that an executive has to face in managing these agencies.

Notes

1

In order to find out how Sargent spent his time, I looked at his daily schedules, divided into fifteen-minute intervals, from 1970 until 1974. This analysis was obviously a rough one because often the calender was changed at the last minute to meet a crisis and the issues considered at appointments with individuals or "staff time" often were not detailed. Still, over the period of four years, such an analysis of the calendar made it possible to arrive at a gross approximation of how the governor spent his time.

2

For documentation of two specific instances of this, see my papers on "Reorganization of Government: the Massachusetts Case" and "Correctional Reform in Massachusetts."

3

Robert Wood, "The Metropolitan Governor," p. 112.

4

Though the leadership styles of political leaders to a certain extent are the result of conscious choices by political executives, it is clear that the issues with which they deal and the style with which they deal with them is often heavily influenced by the publics that are important to them. Leadership style is not only the result of the executive's personal traits but also of his perceptions of public expectations. As Murray Edelman points out in *The Symbolic Uses of Politics* on p. 188:

Through taking the roles of publics whose support they need, public officials achieve and maintain their positions of leadership. The official who correctly gauges the response of publics to his acts, speeches and gestures makes those behaviors significant symbols, evoking common meanings for his audience and for himself and so shaping his further actions as to reassure his public and in this sense "represents" them.

5

The term "technocratic politics" is Samuel H. Beer's, and much of the discussion that follows is based on a helpful conversation with him. The distinction between a "public" issue and a "technocratic" one is not always clear cut. The number of paragovernmental groups in society makes it difficult to enforce this definition strictly. For example, technical advisors who work for government but who advise citizen groups may use their technical skills to clarify a public issue. However, the distinction is useful in trying to determine whether an issue reaches the governor's desk because of immediate public pressure or because it first surfaced within a technical elite and was "translated" into public business.

6

This is one of the points at which the distinction between a governor and his staff becomes obvious. In such a situation, when a staff person is operating as a "minister-without-portfolio" and/or as an advocate, he cannot sustain a large number of losses and still be closely identified as speaking for the governor.

7

For fine documentation of the whole highway moratorium incident, see Alan Lupo, Frank Colcord, and Edmund P. Fowler's *Rites of Way: The Politics of Transportation in Boston and the U.S. City.*

8

For example, the commissioner of public works, Edward Ribbs was fired in the middle of the highway crisis. Robert Ott was replaced by Steven Minter as commissioner of public welfare immediately before the initiation of the flat grant system in the Department of Public Welfare. John Fitzpatrick was replaced by John Boone as commissioner of corrections after the first major uprising at the Massachusetts Correctional Institution at Walpole. Boone was subsequently removed when the prisons continued to flare up.

9

Richard Neustadt, *Presidential Power*, p. 53. Although it is difficult to generalize about personal resources, most students of executive management of large organizations, both public and private, stress their importance. See, for example, James Sterling Young's *The Washington Community 1800-1828*, p. 157ff and Kenneth Andrews' *The Concept of Corporate Strategy*, p. 227ff.

10

For a comparative analysis of the limitations on gubernatorial power see Douglas Fox, *The Politics of City and State Bureaucracy* p. 26ff. It is important to note, however, that Thomas Dye has concluded that "there is little evidence that a governor's formal powers significantly affect policy outcomes in the fifty states." See Thomas Dye, "Executive Power and Public Policy in the United States" in Richard Leach and Timothy O'Rourke, eds., *Dimensions of State and Urban Policymaking*, p. 128.

11

For an excellent analysis of how several presidents arrayed and used their staffs and of the consequences for public policy, see Richard T. Johnson's

"Management Styles of Three U.S. Presidents." One of the points Johnson makes well is that there is no single "best" way to design a political staff, that each style has its costs and benefits.

12

Of all the governors or ex-governors attending the 1974 John F. Kennedy Institute of Politics seminar on "The Governor's Office"—including Hoff of Vermont, Peterson of New Hampshire, Holton of Virginia, Ogilvie of Illinois, and Evans of Washington—only Ogilvie had had a staff of comparable size.

4
**The Department
of Public Works**

The central focus of the reception area of the Massachusetts Department of Public Works (DPW) is a battery of photographs of state and department officials typical of many state agencies. The governor's picture is on a slightly higher level than the photographs of the secretary, commissioner, and associate commissioners. During the Sargent administration what made the DPW's wall of photographs distinctive, however, was that the photograph of Francis Sargent was not the new colored glossy that other state departments displayed but, instead, a slightly dusty and worn picture of a crewcut, much younger Francis Sargent taken when he was commissioner of public works.

One might describe the display of this photograph as symbolic of two important points about the relationship between the governor of Massachusetts and the department. First, Sargent and his predecessor, John Volpe, had both been commissioners of the department and in that sense "one of the DPW team." Second, the department traditionally has regarded its commissioner, not the governor, as the man from whom its personnel take orders. Historically, the department has always been proud of its professional tradition, responsive to a tight hierarchical chain of command and infused with a clear cut sense of mission, namely, construction and maintenance of the Massachusetts network of highways, roads, and bridges.

In order to understand the extent of the governor's control over the Department of Public Works, it is important to look at the organization both as it functioned during the first fifty years of its existence and as it functioned in the late 1960s and early 1970s, when the mission of the department changed significantly. Only by looking at both phases can one understand the organizational character of the department and the extent and kind of its accountability. This chapter is divided into three sections: a description of the department and its personnel and constituents, an analysis of its management in the late 1960s and early 1970s, and an examination of the department's relationship with and accountability to the governor and to other significant individuals and groups. The most important underlying questions of this and subsequent chapters are to what extent the department was managed by the governor and to whom else it was accountable.

The DPW: Background and Description

The origins of the Department of Public Works lie in Governor William Russell's naming of a state highway commission in 1893.[1] The governor's charge to the commission was that it advise him in his efforts to coordinate and supervise the construction and maintenance of the commonwealth's growing network of roads. In 1916 the first Federal Aid Road Act was passed. It provided federal aid to states with the proviso that they coordinate their highway planning. In order for a state to receive funding from the program, it had to have a highway department. In response to this federal requirement and to growing pressures to manage the rapidly burgeoning highway system, the Commonwealth of Massachusetts created the Massachusetts Department of Public Works in 1919.

During the 1940s and 1950s, development of a national network of roads became a high priority for government, with construction and maintenance of roads supported heavily at both the state and federal levels. The Federal Highway Act of 1944 provided for a system of interstate highways, with routes to be determined by state highway departments with federal approval. Emphasis on state highway building reached its peak with the passage of the Federal Highway Act of 1956, which provided that the federal government would supply 90 percent of the funding for construction of interstate roads. Both the federal government and the public had provided the Massachusetts Department of Public Works with a clear cut mandate to construct and maintain the state's roads. Although the department also had responsibility for the state's waterways and for a Bureau of Solid Waste, the major manpower and resources of the department were devoted to highways.

The DPW is directed by a board of commissioners consisting

of one commissioner and four associate commissioners appointed by the governor. Until 1970, when a secretary of transportation was appointed, the commissioner of public works was the ranking transportation official in the government and reported to the governor.[2] The associate commissioners each have a defined area of responsibility for one of four divisions: administrative services, construction, maintenance, and waterways. These associate commissioners may or may not be engineers. This seemingly simple description of responsibility is complicated by the additional hierarchy of professional engineers that reports directly to the commissioner. The senior professional in an administrative position in the department is the chief engineer, who in turn has a whole series of engineering divisions that report to him. The eight district offices of the department are also the responsibility of the chief engineer. Thus, although the responsibility for governing the department technically rests with the commission, the separate hierarchy of the chief engineer and the deputy chief engineers also has considerable influence in the department and has direct access to the commissioner.

Since the 1940s, the department has employed between forty-five hundred and five thousand persons. More than half of them are involved in highway maintenance or construction; more than one-quarter of the total are professional engineers.[3] Of the engineers, most have bachelor's or associate degrees. The department has few engineers with graduate degrees.

Recruitment into the department has occurred in waves.[4] The department hired large numbers of engineers in the late 1920s and early 1930s. In the period between the Depression and World War II the department again hired a large number of employees, and it is from this group that the high-echelon professional nucleus of the department during the Sargent administration was drawn. Since the beginning of the 1950s the department has hired few young people at entrance level positions, both because of the restrictions of the state's civil service system and because of the competition for engineers from firms in the private sector.

The average tenure of department employees in 1974 was approximately twenty-five years.[5] Almost all department personnel are career employees. Many of them have professional training and have worked their way up through the tightly controlled civil service system. In the entire department there are only sixteen positions exempt from civil service, and almost all of these are positions on the commissioner's personal staff. The top engineering policy posts have always been occupied by long-term employees with a strong loyalty to and pride in the professionalism and tradition of the department.

Because of the nature of its funding, the department has traditionally been able to maintain considerable fiscal autonomy and independence from the governor and the legislature. Slightly more than 50 percent of the department's revenues come from the federal government.[6] The department's primary source of revenue for capital expenditures, the Accelerated Highway Fund, is financed by sale of bonds and by direct appropriation based on anticipated federal reimbursement. This is not an annual appropriation but, rather, occurs as frequently as the department and the legislature deem it necessary. Of the $561 million appropriated under the Accelerated Highway Act of 1972, $224 million was requested in the form of bonding authorization. Of the total $561 million, between 70 and 80 percent is reimbursable by the federal government. In 1974 the legislature, acting on its own initiative, added $50 million to the department's request for an authorization of $511 million for aid to localities. In recent years, the legislature has not denied any requests for Accelerated Highway monies but has instead supplemented the DPW budget with its own requests for aid to cities and towns.

The annual operating budget of the department is approximately $80 million. Of the $50 million of this that covers the cost of personnel, about $8 million is federally reimbursable.

The rest of the operating budget is financed through the Highway Maintenance Account, the money received by the state from excise and gasoline taxes. Although the department's operating budget is regularly cut by the governor's office, administration and finance, and the legislature, the department has enjoyed great freedom from cuts with respect to federally aided activity.

The autonomy from state fiscal control the department has traditionally enjoyed is based on the large percentage of the budget that is federal money. One might assume that federal control over the operation of the department would be very tight. In fact, this appears not to have been the case. Most federal highway money Massachusetts has received has come from the Bureau of Public Roads in the Federal Highway Administration (FHWA), a part of the Department of Transportation. Relations between the FHWA and the DPW have always been good. Though the federal government requires that all projects meet strict specifications, the FHWA has done little to interfere with DPW plans for location or size of projects. As the Federal Aid Engineer for the DPW put it, "They (FHWA officials) don't get on our backs much. We interpret the rules and make them come back and tell us we were wrong. We've learned that the worst thing you can do is go to Washington and *ask* for something. We just do it."[7]

This ability to operate freely within the specifications laid down by the federal government has been reinforced by the fact that in most cases the employees of the department in Massachusetts have been working with federal aid longer than their counterparts at the federal level. Most of the negotiations the DPW undertakes with the federal government are handled by the regional offices of FHWA. The FHWA like many other agencies in the federal government, rotates its regional personnel regularly. This fact, coupled with the longevity in their positions of the DPW employees, has often meant that the state's fiscal specialists are regarded as "the experts" by the federal government personnel.

This is not to suggest that the department has functioned independently of the state legislature. There have traditionally been strong ties between the legislature and the department, but this relationship has been one of bargaining rather than of total dependence of the DPW on the legislature. In addition to having a certain amount of fiscal autonomy, the department has traditionally had large numbers of summer and temporary jobs and legislators have always had candidates to fill them. More important, the department provides a variety of services of value to individual representatives. These range from favors of a highly particularistic nature for individual constituents—such as cutting down trees, providing a curbcut, or repairing a particular section of road—to larger favors such as awarding contracts or changing the specifications of dredging, sewage, flood control, or highway projects. Because of such favors, the legislature has traditionally treated the department with care, if not with total deference.

The Department of Public Works is strongly professional, but the department's brand of professionalism is special, if not peculiar. The department could be characterized as influenced by two kinds of professional norms. The first reflects the key role, especially in high policy-making positions, of highway engineers. Their training and experience has been in building highways, and they take great pride in doing it well. Most of the engineers belong to professional engineering societies and even when dealing with contractors and local and federal officials outside the department have most frequent contact with other engineers. The DPW "professional," unlike a doctor or professor, does not act alone but as part of a hierarchical chain of command. The DPW engineers traditionally have not demanded autonomy as a result of their professional training; rather, they adhere to an almost military chain of command. Esteem to an engineer is measured not by the amount of freedom he has in his work but instead by his position in the hierarchy.

This combined sense of hierarchy and professionalism has had two important consequences for the department. First, loyalty of employees has always been directed toward the top professional in the department. As a result, the chief engineer has always been a strong figure. When the commissioner has been an engineer, loyalty to him has been especially strong, bolstered both by respect for the chain of command and also by his importance as the top-ranking professional in the organization.

Another consequence of this "professionalism" is that, to the extent that it dominates, the commissioner or his chief engineer, and not the governor, hold the crucial position at the top of the hierarchy. DPW personnel have traditionally been loyal to the commissioner, even if this loyalty involves being reticent about carrying out the governor's policy.

In addition to having a preponderance of engineers in decision-making positions, the department is also characterized by having a majority of its personnel who are career civil servants. For many of them, a primary concern is the security of their jobs and their advancement up the civil service ladder. Unlike many departments, where the tenure of employees is much shorter, the issues that move them to political action are as often those involving personal security as those involving policy. Many senior officials agreed that Sargent was unpopular with the rank and file of the department. They argued that this was true not only because of his moratorium on highway building and because of his stand on highway policy in general but also because he vetoed pay increases for the department. As Chief Engineer Tierney put it: "I have 4700 employees working for me. On any given policy matter about 500 of them care what the policy is. The one exception, which will have everybody involved, is anything that affects their job status or their pay. That's one way to activate the whole department *very* quickly."[8]

The Management of the DPW

Until the mid-1960s, the Department of Public Works maintained the peculiar autonomy generated by its fiscal independence, its professionalism at doing an easily identifiable task, and its good relationship with the legislature. Gubernatorial control over the department was minimal. As one outside observer of the department in the 1960s put it: "No executive in his right mind seriously challenged the DPW because there was *no* way to control it. Mayor Collins, a highway supporter, would meet with Governor Volpe, and they'd try to iron out what the DPW should do on specific projects. They'd set the agenda—and nothing would happen. So they'd meet again in a few months and go over the same ground. . . ."[9]

Though it is difficult to identify the precise timing or causes of a change in the department's autonomy, it is clear that by the early 1970s the mission or central identifiable motivating force of the department had changed considerably and that the governor and his staff had much more influence over the department's functioning and its policy than they had ever had before. The most important of these changes occurred during the term of Commissioner Edward Ribbs. This is not to suggest that they were caused by Ribbs. Rather, it suggests that Ribbs was at the head of the department during a time of transition and that the governor's refusal to reappoint him marked the end of an era of independence for the Department of Public Works.

Ribbs was appointed commissioner of public works in 1966 by Governor John Volpe to replace newly elected Lieutenant Governor Francis Sargent. Both Volpe, a former commissioner himself, and Sargent played an active part in the recruiting process. To many people, Ribbs seemed the prototype of an ideal DPW commissioner. A native of Boston and an engineer he had worked as a resident engineer in the DPW from 1930 until 1943. In 1943, he joined the Army Corps of Engineers, retiring in 1966 with the rank of brigadier general. With his long experience as an engineer, his belief in a tightly run organization, his close connections with the department, and his total lack of political ambition, he seemed a perfect choice for the job. He returned to an organization in which his colleagues from the 1930s had been promoted into the top professional jobs. He saw his task and the task of the department to be what it had always been—to build highways efficiently and quickly.[10]

The major jobs that lay ahead of Ribbs and the DPW were completion of the Boston area segments of two interstate highways, I-95 and I-93, as well as the construction of the Inner Belt, a circumferential highway within the Greater Boston area. At the same time that Ribbs began to move forward with the construction of the roads, however, a change was beginning to occur in public sentiment in Massachusetts about urban highways.[11] As early as 1966, a small group of citizens and a nonprofit technical advisory group called Urban Planning Aid were beginning to question the proposed location of the Inner Belt through Cambridge. They argued that the route of the Inner Belt, first proposed in the Master Highway Plan of 1948, would destroy a neighborhood unnecessarily and that an alternative route should be considered. The personnel of the Department of Public Works had little sympathy with this argument and continued to plan for construction of the road. Gradually building strength in Cambridge and in other communities, in 1968 the citizen group took their case to the federal highway administrator, Lowell Bridwell, who agreed to order a design and development study to consider alternative alignments for the highway in Cambridge.

The change in people's ideas from the late 1950s about the importance of highways, especially at the expense of settled neighborhoods, seemed to be contagious. By the time Sargent assumed his position as acting governor in 1969, citizen groups in Boston had banded together to form the Greater Boston Coalition (GBC), consisting of Urban Planning Aid and groups from East Boston, Roxbury, the South End, Jamaica Plain, and other communities within the Greater Boston area. They lodged various protests against the Inner Belt, the extensions of I-95 and I-93, the South End bypass, the proposed third harbor crossing, and a variety of other projects that would take land and build roads at the expense of neighborhoods.

Ribbs and other senior DPW officials did not agree with the protesters that the roads should be stopped. They argued that much of the land had already been taken, that it would be illogical to stop building an already partly completed network of roads, that the proposed roads were important in expediting transportation around and through Boston, and that, to a large extent, the economy of the commonwealth depended on the completion of the highway network. They argued that environmental constraints should not be ignored but that they should be tempered by the fiscal limitations on the department. They felt strongly that long-range transportation planning should not be dictated by ephemeral citizen groups. As Ribbs put it: "We felt that we were being confronted with a group of habitual protesters, who move from cause to cause, according to the times. We realized that if you came back to Cambridge or East Boston in ten years, these people would no longer be there. They would have moved on to new causes, leaving the highway planning process in a state of chaos."[12]

The department was not alone in its reluctance to stop progress on the proposed highways. The Chamber of Commerce and much of organized labor felt the roads were necessary, both to meet transportation needs and to ensure the security of the Massachusetts economy. The construction industry was concerned about employment of its workers. In addition, many people, including Donald Dwight, the former associate commissioner of DPW serving as secretary of administration and finance, felt that the commitment had already been made to complete the highway network and that it made little sense to abandon it.

On January 23, 1969, Francis Sargent was sworn in as acting governor to replace John Volpe. On January 25, a large demonstration of citizens protesting the administration's highway policy was held in front of the State House. The issue was a difficult one for Sargent. As the former commissioner of public works who had successfully led the DPW fight for legislation to eliminate the right of localities to veto highways within their jurisdiction and as a former roadbuilder himself, he faced the possibility of alienating an old and familiar constituency. Yet there were powerful counterpressures operating on him. Within his own staff there was disagreement about what should be done. Dwight advocated going ahead with the highway plan. Al Kramer, on the other hand, had begun to be persuaded by the combined arguments of the GBC and his own liberal counterpart in Mayor Kevin White's office, Barney Frank, that there was a case to be made on the other side. Sargent faced an election shortly, and his most likely Democratic opponent, Kevin White, was already beginning to show support for the citizen groups' policies. The issue had reached crisis proportions and seemed certain to have an impact on Sargent's prospects for re-election. He had to act.

In May of 1969, Sargent reached an interim decision, which was to appoint a task force to look at transportation planning in the state. On May 20, he made a speech before the Urban America convention explaining his decision:

Before I gained elective office I was the state's Commissioner for the Department of Public Works, a road builder evolving from a conservationist but determined to perform the tasks of the former with the philosophy of the latter.

But, now, as Governor, it is clear to me we must do more. We must apply the leassons learned in the countryside to the realities of the urban areas. We must, I am saying, challenge the basic assumption of our transportation philosophy. We must, I am saying, review our transportation system, its planning, its effect.[13]

The task force, set up under the chairmanship of Alan Altshuler, a professor of political science from the Massachusetts Institute of Technology, was made up of representatives of a wide variety of disciplines and occupations. The simple fact that the task force was set up at all was a blow to Ribbs and the DPW. The governor for the first time was looking outside his own government for expertise on highway planning. This became even more painful for the department as it became clear that Altshuler and the task force were more impressed with their own ability to reason out what should be done than with the DPW's. As Altshuler put it:

As we came to the end of November, the task force had been radicalized. The protesters had made a better case than the officials. We spent a lot of time with Ribbs and his colleagues. . . We thought they had made a very inadequate defense of their plans.

The task force was more professional with respect to planning than the DPW, whose top officials are construction engineers, not planners. . . They [the DPW] apparently had been uninterested in planning studies, which they regarded as a necessity imposed on them by federal law.[14]

The task force reported to Sargent on January 8, 1970, urging that work be halted on the Inner Belt, the Route 2 extension, and the Southwest Expressway. The option of declaring a moratorium had not been included in the task force's original mandate—they had arrived at it through their own study process and because of steadily increasing salience of the community groups' points of view. In making their report to the governor, they labeled state highway planning a "pathological planning and decision process" and said that "we find on the one hand extreme citizen distrust of the DPW, on the other extreme DPW rigidity, defensiveness, and insensitivity to broad political and planning values."[15]

In February of 1970, after much heated discussion among his staff, Sargent went on television to announce a moratorium on most of the highway building that had been opposed and to propose that a significant restudy of the state's total transportation needs be undertaken. In the spring of 1971, Sargent named Alan Altshuler as the state's first secretary of transportation and construction. One of Altshuler's conditions for taking the job was that Ribbs not be reappointed to another term.

The decision to remove Ribbs was not an easy one for Sargent. Business and labor, most of the legislature, and a host of other groups that had long been powerful in state affairs supported Ribbs. Sargent had helped recruit him. The department was loyal to him. In a sense, he would not only be removing Ribbs but also relieving the department of its traditional way of looking at the world. Ribbs had staunchly stood up for what he understood to be his mandate when he took the job. The department's objectives and policies and Ribbs's survival had become issues not because the department had in any way changed the way it had been operating for twenty years, but because Sargent had changed his own position when he felt that he had to "manage" a crisis. The department still performed well at what its personnel thought it was supposed to do. It was Sargent who sensed the possibility of political disaster if he remained a roadbuilder and who consequently found it imperative to change the nature of the transportation planning process. He had no means at his disposal to change the department short of removing Ribbs from office. Although after the moratorium Sargent ordered Ribbs to stop leveling houses in preparation for the highways, the department continued to knock them down. To make matters worse, Sargent had only a limited amount of staff time that he could devote to managing the department. The time required to stop the department from going its own way was enormous. As one staff member put it:

We had to run the department from the State House on a day-to-day basis. They would do something they weren't supposed to do, like demolish buildings, and we'd have to figure out some way to stop them. They'd submit legislation to allow them to move on a right-of-way. We'd have to issue a rule telling them to submit all of their legislation through our office. We'd tell them to do something and nothing would happen—so we'd have to find out why. It was absolute bedlam. We couldn't keep it up.[16]

Sargent accepted Ribbs's resignation in 1971. The initiative to change the policy direction of the department had come from Sargent rather than from the department itself. He in turn had been activated by public pressure. Because "managing" the department in this case involved stopping the department from carrying on its operations, the actual enforcement of his decision was not as difficult as initiation of a new policy might have been. The decision of what to do about the DPW was his to make and the need to take action was clear. He perceived the issue of highway planning and implementation as crucial to his political survival. The department's resistance became a secondary issue. He had to advocate new policies of citizen participation and "balanced" transportation although by doing so he faced DPW opposition. The fact that he relied on outside expertise to help him make this decision only served to make it even more difficult for the department to accept.

It was not only the result of the controversy between the governor and the department over the Inner Belt and the interstates that led to the department's change of mission in the late 1960s and early 1970s, however. Several other important and often interlocking changes were occurring at the same time. Perhaps most important was a movement in public opinion throughout the country away from supporting automobiles and highways as the solution to the problem of urban transportation. Federal aid began to be directed to mass transit as well as to highways. In 1964, Congress funded the Urban Mass Transit Administration, which provided $4 million in its first year for mass transit in Massachusetts. In 1973, the federal government agreed that a certain portion of interstate monies could be "swapped" for use on other transportation priorities. The rhetoric of personnel at the federal Department of Transportation, created in 1967, began to change from emphasizing the completion of the interstate system to stressing "balanced transportation." Government investment in transportation continued to increase throughout the 1960s, but the mix of services changed. In Massachusetts between 1964 and 1968, the average annual investment in transportation was $91 million.[17] Between 1969 and 1973, this average figure increased to $148 million per year. During the mid-1960s, only negligible amounts of this investment were devoted to transit. Between 1969 and 1973, investment in transit accounted for 25 percent of the total.

Accompanying the federal emphasis on balanced transportation were demands at all levels that highway planning have citizen participation and that highway plans be environmentally sound. Federal funding was often contingent on meeting minimum guidelines for both. This fact alone robbed the DPW of a good deal of the autonomy in locating and designing roads that it had traditionally enjoyed. As the chief engineer of the department put it:

In all candor, I'm not sure that even if the governor had allowed us to work on the Southwest Expressway, we would have been able to do it. The environmental constraints were tough enough and the number of citizen veto groups mandated to participate in the process were widespread enough that I'm not sure we could have put up a close facsimile to what they demanded and still have hit within millions of a reasonable budget.[18]

The responsiveness of the legislature to the department had also changed. Although the department still was able to grant valuable favors to representatives, many of the once plentiful patronage jobs in the department had dried up. In addition, many legislators, like the rest of the public, had begun to regard the idea that highways were unequivocally good with suspicion. As the chief legislative liaison for the DPW put it: "Transportation issues have become strange in the past few years. We have a new breed of legislator, one who certainly doesn't regard building highways as a partisan issue, or even as an issue on which he has to come down on the same side time and time again. They seem to decide almost on an issue-by-issue basis."[19]

The department's change of mission was also caused to a certain degree by the fact that many of the department's oldest employees, who came to the department during the Depression, were eligible for retirement. Many of those who could have stayed on for a few more years retired because of the shift in emphasis in the department. In addition, several of the top policy jobs in the department were being allocated to planners rather than to engineers. The line between being a planner and being an engineer in the department had become a distinct one. As one young engineer who took on a planning job put it: "In moving from an engineering job into this one, I've burned some bridges behind me. The attitude around here is that once you've become a pickle, you can never be a cucumber again."[20]

A final important shift in the nature of the department occurred when the new position of secretary of transportation and construction was created. The positions of the cabinet secretaries were created by the governor and the legislature to allow functional specialists responsible to the governor to be in charge of a cluster of related agencies and to monitor and manage their administration. Altshuler took his mandate seriously. He had developed considerable expertise in transportation as the chairman of the Governor's Task Force on Transportation. He had made Ribbs's resignation a condition for his taking the job and after Ribbs's departure recommended that the governor appoint Bruce Campbell, an engineer unswervingly loyal to Altshuler. He also placed loyalists in several key positions in the department and on his own staff in the secretariat.

He tightly centralized the decision-making process in the department so that all important decisions came before him. He also worked hard to gain the full confidence of the governor's staff to ensure a key role for himself in the policy-making process. He actively attempted to control the behavior of the department's employees. He did this largely through his use of Campbell as an intermediary. At the same time he consciously tried to formulate and influence the transportation policies that the department and his secretariat were responsible for carrying out. As Ribbs had been, he was a constant presence in department meetings, but he also used his position as secretary to become the governor's main transportation planner and enjoyed his confidence and support. The senior officials of the DPW met weekly with Altshuler to consider and discuss both major and minor matters affecting the department. Altshuler presided at these meetings and made the final decisions about what action should be taken. The chain of command from the governor's office to the department was clear not only on paper, but in fact. All major policy decisions funneled through the secretary's office. The governor's staff looked to Altshuler's office both for advice on all DPW matters and to enforce any decisions on DPW matters that they wished to make. Unlike the DPW of an earlier era, the department's lines of accountability and obligation to the governor's office were explicit and enforced, though this was due more to Altshuler's being able successfully to wedge himself between the department and the governor than to any particular effort on the governor's part.

Altshuler's first priority when he took office in 1971 was to place his own choices in key positions in the department, the most crucial of which was the job of the commissioner. According to Altshuler, he had seen enough of the department to understand that the new commissioner would have to be a professional engineer:

As far as the career people in the DPW were concerned, I was a professor of political science. I needed a comrade, but one with professional credentials which would be respected. I was operating on the assumption that the professional societies were reachable, that they were significant as opinion leaders, and that many of the most competent engineers in the department would respond to a commissioner who was also a first-rate engineer.[21]

Soon after Altshuler's appointment as secretary, Sargent offered the job of commissioner to Bruce Campbell. This proved to be a crucial appointment. Campbell was a highway engineer and former head of the Massachusetts Safety Council. His specialty had been traffic management and safety rather than construction. His professional ties were long and strong and he was well regarded by much of the DPW's old constituency of engineers, contractors, and labor. In 1958 he had written a paper arguing, contrary to what most people believed at the time, that the entire interstate highway system would not be built because it would not be capable of accommodating all the traffic that would want to use it or of providing a totally acceptable transportation option for the cities. When the debate over extension of the highway network began to heat up in the late 1960s, Campbell maintained his keen interest in how the interstate system should be built. As program chairman for the Institute of Traffic Engineers, he ran a series of luncheon meetings on the controversy and began to attend the public meetings being held to discuss the completion of the highway network. It was here that he encountered Altshuler. As Campbell explains it:

Altshuler was making the same arguments that I was about the feasibility of the highways, but he was making them on different grounds. I had said that the numbers and financing of the highway system wouldn't work. He was looking at credits and debits, but at the credits and debits to people. He was asking "what are the impacts?"

I became convinced that my view had been too narrow, that my notion of costs had been too limited. Despite the fact that I knew that there were fine people in the DPW, I became convinced that the direction of the department was wrong. At the time, I had ambitions to be the first secretary of transportation myself, but I had to admit honestly that Altshuler would be better. I decided early in the controversy that I wanted to work for him.[22]

Campbell came into the department with a well thought out philosophy about the job of commissioner, a philosophy shared by Altshuler.

I had to be a professional to run the department. I knew the key people and I knew the answers to their arguments because I'd been in the field for years. The two arguments that they'd use to question any change in plans were those of safety and those of "capacity." As an engineer, I understood what those meant, and I could counter them.

I knew that I also had to make some key appointments of my own, but that to do anything big we'd have to produce it through the civil service employees, to make them go along with us. To do this we had to make them understand that we're a service agency—that we don't set policy, but instead help to implement it. The governor sets policy, Alan carries it out, and the department helps him. I consider my job to be enforcement of this policy, while keeping as many of the trivial details of administration of the department off Altshuler's desk as possible.[23]

Altshuler's choice of Campbell as commissioner served several important functions. It assured him of having a highly regarded professional who could deal with some elements of the department that were hostile to Altshuler because of his stand on the highway controversy and because he was not an engineer. At the same time, he had selected a commissioner whose loyalty to Altshuler was unquestionable and who viewed the commissioner's job as that of implementing the governor's and the secretary's priorities.

This grafting of the professional loyalty of the department to the office of the commissioner and the secretary was further cemented by the choice by Altshuler and Campbell of Robert Tierney for the job of chief engineer of the DPW. When Campbell took office, Tierney was one of five deputy-chiefs. He had served in the department for more than twenty years. He was esteemed both as an engineer and as a supervisor although he was the only one of the five deputy chiefs who had been opposed to the construction of the Inner Belt. Like many previous incumbents in the job of chief engineer, he was unswerving in his loyalty to the commissioner and to the department. His appointments provided a second strong link between the career professionals in the department and the secretary's office.

Altshuler's control and influence over the department was enhanced by his early decisions to put individuals who were both professionally respected and loyal to him into central positions. Several other factors were also crucial in strengthening Altshuler's control over the department. The most important of these was the fact that Altshuler and Campbell came into their jobs with an idea of their priorities and with a sense of a timetable for accomplishing these priorities that proved fortuitous. Altshuler came to the post of secretary with clear directions from the governor's office to deal with highway policy. The decision to stop the highways had been articulated recently and clearly by the governor. Though as secretary Altshuler was responsible for other agencies and authorities, the DPW had to be the primary focus for his attention, both because of the implications of the policies with which it was dealing and because of its size in comparison with the other parts of the secretariat. Unlike many of the state's other secretaries, his attention and that of his staff was focused on one department. Much of Altshuler's own staff had worked with him since he chaired the Governor's Task Force, and they shared his sense of priorities. The secretariat and the department had two clear jobs as a result of the controversy of the previous five years: to oversee the successful conduct of the Boston Transportation Planning Review (the group that had since the governor's highway moratorium re-studied the entire transportation planning process for Boston) and to develop a method of ensuring citizen participation in the transportation planning process.[24] Focusing on both of these priorities meant focusing on the DPW and doing so at a time when members of the department who had been building high-ways for thirty years were not certain of what their job was. The traditional DPW was to be no more, a fact that was most pointedly illustrated by the secretary's recommendation to eliminate the department as a separate unit in his proposal for reorganization legislation submitted to the legislature in 1972. Altshuler's staff and Campbell's staff were not only prepared to tell the department *what* they wanted the DPW to do but also to devote considerable staff time to making certain that they did it.

Altshuler's and Campbell's establishment of a list of priorities was also notable for what it did *not* include and for what they did not take on. Their goals were explicit, clearly stated, and measurable. They did not suggest that their goal was to make the department "more efficient" or "more productive" or that they wanted to infuse the department with a raft of new per-sonnel. As one senior official of the secretariat put it:

We recognized that we were dealing with a ponderous, inefficient depart-ment. We had thousands doing the work of hundreds. But we came into the whole thing realizing that we couldn't change the entire Massachusetts state government overnight. We knew that we could bring in some of our own people but that basically we'd have to make the system that we had work for us. We found as many good career people as we could. We said what we wanted to do and accepted certain inefficiencies with an air of resignation. If we had spent all of our energy on achieving some grandiose notions of efficiency, we would have threatened the hell out of the depart-ment. They would have gone to battle with us when their security was threatened, and we probably would have lost.[25]

The fact that the commissioner and the secretary clearly articulated their goals and devoted their attention to imple-menting them at a time when the DPW was changing rapidly helped place the department in the position of needing to turn to the commissioner and the secretary for guidance and direction.

The Governor and the DPW

Altshuler took the initiative to build a strong relationship between his office and the governor's office. In return, he enjoyed support, both public and private, from the governor and his staff. This was important because it caused the governor's office to delegate policy-making authority to Altshuler. It also helped spread widely the impression that Altshuler had the governor's full confidence, a fact that allowed him to be influential in dealing both with the department and with other transportation constituencies. The strength and closeness of Altshuler's relationship to the governor and his staff and their confidence in him was the result of several factors. He understood both the technical problems of his job and the political climate in which he had to operate. He had worked with the governor's office for as long as the issue of highway planning and citizen participation in it had been a political issue. His work on issues was meticulous and accurate. His own style of management was geared more to anticipating issues by involving himself in details than to handling crises. This meant that he did not compete with the governor and his staff to generate and manage crises. Altshuler's earliest supporter in the governor's office, Al Kramer, remained in a position of authority during Sargent's term and remained an Altshuler admirer and patron. Among the senior members of the governor's staff, Altshuler enjoyed the reputation of being among the most capable of all ten of the secretaries, a judgment shared by a good many of the staff of the Executive Office of Transportation and Construction and of the DPW.

This reputation built on itself. Confidence in Altshuler's abilities was enhanced in the governor's office by the fact that there were no major crises in the field of transportation after Altshuler took office. This helped him retain control in two ways.

First, he was perceived throughout the government as not having caused any crises and therefore keeping his secretariat "under control." Second, he was universally regarded as having a good understanding of technical day-to-day management issues. Because there were no issues of crisis proportions for the governor, Sargent and his staff did not feel they had to involve themselves intimately in the decision making of the secretariat.

Equally important in understanding the high regard of the governor and his staff for Altshuler is the fact that he and his commissioner of public works were considered among the most loyal to the governor of all the administrative officials in state government. The crucial test of this loyalty had occurred early in Altshuler's tenure as secretary. The Boston Transportation Planning Review (BTPR) made its report to the governor in a meeting that included Altshuler, John Wofford (the director of the BTPR), and senior members of the governor's staff. Altshuler urged that construction of several four-lane special-purpose highways be allowed in exception to a general rule of no more highway construction. He argued that the absolute merit of a decision to stop all highways was certainly not clear, and that it would be a mistake to decide the issue because of a wave of antihighway hysteria.[26] Kramer and Wofford opposed the decision and won the governor's approval of their position. Altshuler was charged with writing the governor's speech on the subject and with carrying out the policy. As one participant in the meeting put it: "Writing the governor's statement on that policy was significant for Alan. You could almost see him painfully testing how important the issue was to him as he went along. By the time he had written it, he was convinced that it was certainly not an issue worth resigning over and that it was therefore one which he could and must support."[27] After the policy was decided, he worked hard to implement it, lobbying for it both around the state and in Washington. As Altshuler himself summed it up:

That decision strengthened me in the governor's office. They know that I've rested my authority on my relationship to the governor. I have told the governor that I have found it easy to give him such loyalty because his decisions have always reflected a conscientious effort to balance the pros and cons, and his actions have always been characterized by total integrity and fundamental human decency. Clearly, and I have told him this too, if I ever found myself working for a chief executive who was making base decisions, I would consider it my duty to object and resign.[28]

Neither Altshuler nor Campbell had ambitions to hold elective office. Neither deliberately cultivated a personal constituency separate from the governor's. From Altshuler's own description of his relationship to constituencies it is clear that he had thought about it a great deal and had taken a calculated stand:

I have no constituency of my own except those people who support me in carrying out the governor's policy. I have to develop policies which have constituencies, but I have about as much of a personal following as Walter Hickel had before he resigned. People know that I won't push transportation projects down their throats. But I haven't sought to be loved by particular groups. Many administrators see the "friends" and the "enemies" on all issues and want to be with the "friends." I'd rather be widely acceptable but not loved.[29]

This loyalty and lack of personal political ambition on Altshuler's part was widely acknowledged by the governor's staff. It was because of this loyalty and because of the governor's admiration for Altshuler's abilities that, unlike any of the other secretariats (except the Executive Office of Administration and Finance), the entire Executive Office of Transportation and Construction and its agencies had no member of the governor's staff assigned to oversee their functioning. In effect, Altshuler doubled as secretary of transportation and as the governor's chief transportation staff advisor. No one except the governor himself had the power, formal or informal, to overrule Altshuler's decisions.

Perhaps the best way to describe the policy-making process in the DPW as it developed under Altshuler is as most frequently controlled by the secretary with the concurrence of the governor and his staff and of the senior staff of the DPW. The major "crisis decision," to stop the highways, had already been made by the governor. Day-to-day management was left to Altshuler and Campbell. During the early 1970s, the links between a previously relatively autonomous department and an often helpless governor's office were tightened considerably. This was the result both of Altshuler's conscious effort to control the department and of the change in the department itself.

Dealings between the governor's office and the department during Altshuler's tenure always involved Altshuler. Neither Commissioner Campbell nor his subordinates ever met with the governor without Altshuler present. From 1972 until the end of Sargent's term, the Executive Office of Transportation served as a management floodgate, regulating the flow of issues between the governor's office and the DPW, making decisions on some issues and passing others on to the other side for further work or discussion. This style of management was characteristic on a variety of issues. Many of the mundane policy issues that bubbled up from the department were settled by Altshuler at his weekly meetings with the senior DPW staff. For example, questions of highway maintenance or lighting or redirection of traffic flow while major roads were being repaired were discussed and resolved without being referred to the governor's office at all.

Other kinds of issues that surfaced either in the DPW or in the secretariat but that required action by the governor were also handled primarily in the secretary's office. For example, in 1973 Sargent was asked by Altshuler to lobby in Washington for Congress to allow monies earmarked for the construction of the interstate system to be used to develop other forms of transportation. Contact with the governor's office was handled by the secretariat and the staff work done on the issue coordinated by Altshuler. Though the DPW was involved in the process and had a distinct stake in the outcome, both the policy and the logistics were worked out in Altshuler's office. The Executive Office of Transportation and Construction also handled all major contacts with both the legislature and the federal government.

Because Sargent devoted none of his own staff resources to transportation and because of the high esteem in which he held Altshuler, Sargent and his immediate staff made very few attempts to initiate policy for the Department of Public Works. The secretariat and the department were responsible for initiation of policy and for calling these policies to Sargent's attention when they were significant. The one instance of a governor's staff member attempting to change a department policy occurred when a junior staff member urged the secretary and the department to reopen a wrong-way bus lane that had been closed after a member of the DPW maintenance crew was killed while working on the road. Although the staff man spent a considerable amount of time, with the support of his superiors, in the governor's office urging Altshuler and Campbell to reopen the bus lane immediately, Campbell and Altshuler remained unconvinced by his arguments and the lane remained closed until the following spring.

Issues that involved the DPW occasionally became immediately publicly visible and required action on the part of the governor as well as a technical judgment on the part of the DPW. For example, when the Mystic River Bridge, the major means of access to the North Shore, collapsed when struck by a truck in the summer of 1973, the governor's office had to issue statements about how the crisis would be handled. Although the instructions were announced from the governor's office, the judgments on how to reroute traffic were made within the DPW and the secretariat. The only policy instruction that came from the governor's office was that the department and secretariat could do anything they deemed advisable as long as it did not get the governor into political trouble.

The kind of issue that puts the greatest strain on the relationship between a department and the governor's office, namely one on which a governor must take a strong stand because his political survival is at stake, did not arise in the DPW after 1972, when the governor made his decision on the highway moratorium. A transportation issue of crisis proportion had dictated that Sargent and his staff become actively involved in making departmental policy. After that decision was made, no crises arose. Even if they had arisen, Altshuler would have remained a key decision maker and highly influential. Sargent regarded him as one of his most loyal and closest advisors and had developed no competing source of expertise on his own staff. Altshuler was known to be capable of making the DPW perform. The department was firmly loyal to Campbell and Campbell to Altshuler. As one senior official put it: "The last major policy decision in transportation in which Alan Altshuler had no say was the question of whether he should be appointed secretary or whether he had outlived his political usefulness. From then on, he couldn't be excluded."[30]

The DPW's relationship to the governor changed during the 1970s. Before then the department moved along on its own course, with little direction or attempt at direction from the governor's office. By 1974, the department had become increasingly responsive to the policy laid down by the governor's office and mediated by a strong secretary. This was partly the result of Altshuler's willingness to handle both technical and mundane details of the department's functioning while remaining completely loyal to Sargent. In addition, it was the result of the nature of the department itself. Ironically, many of the same qualities that bolstered the department's autonomy before the 1960s were responsible for making the department responsive to a commissioner and a secretary who were, in turn, responsive to the governor. The respect for hierarchy and willingness to work their way up through the ranks of the engineers among the career civil servants in the department meant that there was little or no end-running of the commissioner or the secretary. The strong sense of loyalty to a professional commissioner, which made it almost impossible for Sargent to deal with Ribbs in the 1960s, was put to work in the governor's favor in the 1970s.

In addition, the very fact that a change of goals and of mission was such a traumatic experience for the department meant that new goals clearly articulated by the governor through his designated manager were grasped onto by the department, allowing it to retain many of its career personnel and much of its organizational distinctiveness while its energies were directed to a new end. Finally, the department was used to functioning with a clear task. Sargent responded to a crisis with a decision to change what that task was. He had been publicly successful at doing this because his decision had had considerable citizen support and because it had involved opposition to an ongoing program. It was clear both to Altshuler and to department personnel that their first priority was to stop building roads. Altshuler took advantage of the clarity of this priority and of the department's strong sense of hierarchy to issue explicit orders about how the department was to run and what it was supposed to do. Although its mission had changed, the DPW responded, as it always had, to orders that were both publicly articulated and clear. Sargent, in turn, received widespread acclaim for having made a department that was "unmanageable" in the 1960s more responsive to him and to the public.

Notes

1

The department held a seventy-fifth anniversary celebration in 1968. Most of the early history of the department was furnished to me by Daniel O'Leary, assistant to the commissioner of public works. Robert S. Friedman's essay on "State Politics and Highways" was also helpful for general history of American public works departments.

2

I will discuss the results of the creation of the secretary's position later. The major structural change that occurred was to make the commissioner report *through* the secretary to the governor. The organization below the level of commissioner of public works has remained the same despite the creation of the secretariat.

3

These statistics were supplied to me by Robert Tierney, the chief engineer in the DPW. Though the department maintains few official records on kinds of personnel, officials of the department have done internal studies, on which I have relied heavily in the following paragraphs.

4.

Ibid.

5

This figure was supplied to me by Bernie Levitta, assistant to the chief engineer. Although it is only an approximation, it is based on retirement data and projections that most senior officials of the department assume to be accurate.

6

Interview with George Joseph, federal aid engineer. Most of the fiscal information contained in the following paragraphs was supplied by Joseph.

7

Ibid.

8

Interview with Robert Tierney.

9

Interview with Fred Salvucci, transportation advisor to the mayor of Boston and former transportation advisor to the Boston Redevelopment Authority.

10

Interview with Edward Ribbs.

11
I will not attempt to describe in any detail the rise of citizen opposition to the completion of the highways or the political battle that ensued. Two excellent studies of the highway controversy are Alan Lupo, Frank Colcord, and Edmund P. Fowler, *Rites of Way* and Ralph Gakenheimer, "Technics and Conflict: The Open Study in Urban Transportation." This study has been published as *Transportation Planning as Response to Controversy: Participation and Conflict in the Boston Case.*

12
Interview with Edward Ribbs.

13
Francis Sargent, quoted in Lupo, Colcord, and Fowler, *Rites of Way*, p. 68.

14
Alan Altshuler, quoted in ibid., p. 91.

15.
Task Force report, quoted in ibid., p. 95.

16
Interview with a senior member of the governor's staff.

17
Figures from a speech by Alan Altshuler, March 6, 1974, to the Boston Citizen Seminar on Transportation Plans and Planning for the Future (typewritten).

18
Interview with Robert Tierney.

19
Interview with Jerry Conway, legislative liaison for the Department of Public Works.

20
Interview with Tom Humphrey, fiscal planner in the Bureau of Transportation Planning and Development, DPW.

21
Interview with Alan Altshuler.

22
Interview with Bruce Campbell, commissioner of public works.

23
Ibid.

24
Interview with Alan Altshuler.

25
Interview with a senior member of the staff of the Executive Office of Transportation and Construction who asked not to be quoted by name.

26
Interview with Alan Altshuler.

27
Interview with DPW Associate Commissioner John Wofford.

28
Interview with Alan Altshuler.

29
Ibid.

30
Interview with a senior official of the Executive Office of Transportation and Construction who asked not to be quoted by name.

5
The Department of Public Welfare

During his six years as governor, Francis Sargent was "responsible" for the management of more than two hundred separate state agencies, boards, and commissions. Of all of these, the single agency he was most frequently criticized for "mismanaging" was the Department of Public Welfare. As in other states, public concern over public welfare increased dramatically in Massachusetts in the 1960s. The governor and the state administration became the focal points for this concern when, in 1968, the state assumed administrative control of the welfare system from the local offices that had administered it since the system began. By 1970, the governor's control and administration of the multimillion-dollar welfare system had become a major election issue and a widely debated and emotion-laden issue of public policy.

Perhaps the most important feature of the Department of Public Welfare is that its tasks are extremely diverse and complex and almost impossible to articulate. On this point, the welfare department differed significantly from the Department of Public Works during the time that Sargent was governor. Though public works involved the governor in several crucial political battles, the issue at stake during the Sargent administration revolved around one simple question—whether or not to build a particular road or set of roads. There was no correspondingly clear-cut issue for the Department of Public Welfare during the Sargent years. Welfare's goals were diverse, difficult to measure, and varied from program to program. In addition, in recent years public welfare has acquired a peculiar public and emotional significance that has made it a lightning rod for many hopes and fears not even remotely related to the actual administration or programs of the department. The nature of the department's "task," combined with the unique history and structure of the department, have to a great extent defined the kinds of management of the department that any governor can do, as well as the nature of the audience to whom the department must respond.

This chapter is divided into three sections. The first section is a brief description of the Department of Public Welfare as it was during the Sargent administration, with a glance backward at the events of historical significance that affected the structure of the department. The second section is an examination of the goals, priorities, and responses to outside stimuli of the department and of how these were "managed" from 1969 on. The final section describes several issues that arose during the term of two welfare commissioners and on which the governor and his staff attempted to exercise control over the department. It also looks at why the relationship between the department and Sargent was what it was and at what gubernatorial management of the department meant.

The Department of Public Welfare: Background and Description

The Massachusetts Department of Public Welfare is one of the state's oldest and largest departments. The department's budget request consistently represents approximately 40 percent of the governor's total budget submission. In the 1975 fiscal year that request was for a little over $1 billion.

The chief administrator of the department is the commissioner. He is appointed by the governor and serves a coterminous term with him. The department falls directly under the jurisdiction of the Executive Office of Human Services (EOHS), the umbrella agency for several of the state's largest "service-providing" departments. Unlike the heads of many other Massachusetts administrative agencies, the commissioner of public welfare is not the chairman of a board of commissioners but functions as the sole responsible executive of the department. One deputy commissioner, five assistant commissioners, one director, and several members of his personal staff report directly to the commissioner. The deputy commissioner has been granted life tenure in his job by the legislature. The other central staff appointments are subject to civil service requirements and regulations. Each assistant commissioner is responsible for one of the five divisions of the department: administration, research and planning, field operations, social services, and medical assistance. Additional senior positions include those for a director of administrative services and a regional coordinator as well as several personal assistants to the commissioner. During most of the Sargent administration this senior staff functioned in a collegial manner on most major questions of welfare policy, and it was often difficult to tell from titles where responsibility for a given issue lay. The state is divided into seven welfare regions, each with a director who reports to the regional coordinator in the central office. The directors of the state's 122 local welfare offices and community service centers are responsible to one of the seven regional directors.

The department officially came into existence in 1919, though as early as 1675 Massachusetts had assumed financial responsibility for the "nonsettled" poor who fled to Boston as a result of King Philip's War. Though "poor relief" was considered primarily a local responsibility, the state enacted a "mother's aid" program in 1914 and assumed responsibility for those in need of assistance who had not satisfied the residence requirements in any city or town.[1] With the enactment of the Social Security Act in 1935, the federal government authorized grants to the states for the aged, the blind, and dependent children. Massachusetts in turn passed on this money with a significant state supplement to the localities, enforcing federal standards and promulgating its own rules for localities on how the state share should be used. In the 1950s and 1960s, as new programs of assistance such as those for the disabled (DA) and those for the medically indigent (MAA) were added to the list of federal programs, the state increased the total financial share it contributed to welfare programs. By 1963, when the state assumed part of the cost of general relief, there were no public welfare programs to which the state did not make some contribution.

As Massachusetts began to finance increasing numbers of welfare programs, the legislature began to promulgate rules and regulations stipulating how these programs should be administered.

By the 1960s, the state department had authority to hear appeals, establish criteria for size of offices, set qualifications for local administrators, and regulate standards for assistance. However, the department was still unable to affect the appointment of local office directors, many of whom were prominent local politicians or their friends. In addition, though in theory the state department had considerable power to promulgate rules and to enforce them, in fact the department had neither the staff nor the incentives necessary to regulate the behavior of local offices.

Through the mid-1960s local offices had considerable autonomy in operating and in determining who was eligible for assistance. The result was that both the level of financial assistance and the quality of programs varied widely in different locations in the state. The state department theoretically had the right to withhold funds from localites, but it very rarely used this power. By 1965, a group of reformers, mostly from among private service organizations and "good government" groups, were demanding an end to this uneven treatment; and in 1968 the state Department of Public Welfare assumed control over all public assistance functions, including the newly passed federal Medicaid program.

The welfare department administers several categories of aid, each of which has a distinct set of clienteles and program goals and standards. The largest category of expenditures in the welfare budget is Medicaid, the state's single most expensive program. Created to provide assistance to the medically needy, the Medicaid program provides services and funds to more than six-hundred thousand persons per year, at a cost in the 1974 fiscal year of more than $400 million.[2] Medicaid pays not only for expenses of those covered by other welfare categories but also for those whose medical expenses exceed their ability to pay them. This often includes assumption of the cost of hospitals, nursing homes, drugs, and outpatient services for victims of catastrophic illness as well as regular medical treatment for those who fall into other public assistance categories and "the poor." The federal government provides 50 percent reimbursement for most Medicaid cases, and the state pays the other 50 percent.

The second largest and most controversial category of public assistance is Aid to Families with Dependent Children (AFDC). AFDC provides a cash grant to children under eighteen and the adults responsible for them if the family is unable to support itself. It accounted for more than $300 million of the department's appropriation for the 1974 fiscal year, of which the federal government paid 50 percent. Most of this $300 million is spent on direct cash payments to recipients, but it also includes some monies for such social services as homemaker services, counseling, and family planning.

The department also provides a variety of services to children, including group care and foster care (for those removed from their homes by the state) and adoption services. Until the 1960s these programs were administered by a separate division of the welfare department, the Division of Child Guardianship, the most highly professionalized division of the department. These programs have also always had a strong constituency outside the department, including many private service providers and various child advocacy groups. These services account for more than $45 million and are 75 percent reimbursable by the federal government.

The three other major categorical programs the state supports are General Relief (GR), Disability Assistance (DA), and Old Age Assistance (OAA). General Relief, funded entirely by state monies, is designed to make a cash payment to those who do not fall into any other assistance category but who do not have enough money to survive. In the 1974 and 1975 fiscal years the cost of GR was more than $60 million. In 1974 the federal government assumed responsibility for administration of both OAA and DA. Under this system the federal government makes a basic grant in each category, which the states may then supplement. Because Massachusetts grants before the federal takeover were higher than the federal minimum, the department pays a supplement to the federal government that it then adds on to the checks it mails out. In the 1974 and 1975 fiscal years the state share of these two programs was almost $100 million.

The federal government provides between 40 and 50 percent of the total dollars spent on public assistance in Massachusetts.[3] Because of this and because of the voluminous and detailed regulations the federal government has spelled out for each program, the federal government's role in the politics of welfare is significant.[4] For each categorical assistance program (and in many cases for subcategories) the state must submit a plan to the federal government to which both the state and the federal government must agree. In addition to working on the details of the plan, the federal government attempts to influence both the quality and the equity of state programs by issuing detailed regulations and by conducting audits and inspections.

The two major federal departments with which the Massachusetts department deals are the Department of Health, Education and Welfare (HEW) and for food supplements and food stamps, the Department of Agriculture. Most of the federal money that Massachusetts receives comes from the Social and Rehabilitation Service (SRS) of HEW, though increasingly in recent years as the federal government has taken over payment functions for various categories of assistance, the department has had to deal with the Social Security Administration. SRS remains the major federal bureau with which the welfare department has to transact business, however, both because of the amount of money it contributes to Massachusetts programs and because of the discretionary nature of the programs it administers.

The day-to-day administration of SRS is handled in regional offices, and it is with the regional office that welfare department officials most frequently deal. Unlike the Department of Public Works, the Department of Public Welfare's contacts with Washington are infrequent, and personal ties between state and federal officials are remote. From the early 1960s on, the HEW structure of bureaus and organizations in Washington has changed frequently, with a relatively high turnover of personnel. The regional office, meanwhile, has retained many of the same personnel over the years, a large percentage of whom are social workers with program backgrounds rather than with management training. With the advent of the Nixon administration, the emphasis of the Washington-based officials of HEW was on fiscal management and austerity rather than on program innovation. This meant that the regional offices, with their old staffs of program specialists, played an increasingly minor role in decision making on federal government welfare policy.

These factors had several consequences for the Massachusetts welfare department in the early 1970s. The Massachusetts department's staff, like that of the regional office, was made up of many professional social workers who had made a career of social welfare administration. Their ties to the regional office were strong, but this had little effect on funding decisions in Washington because the authority of the regional offices had declined.[5] The career welfare staff in Massachusetts also shared the low morale of the regional offices because they saw older program specialists like themselves being replaced by fiscal experts. Finally, because turnover was rapid in Washington during Nixon's term and because Elliot Richardson, a "friend" of the Massachusetts welfare system, left his job as secretary of HEW, the relationships between both political and administrative officials in Massachusetts and Washington became tenuous. Unlike the relationship between the Department of Public Works and the Federal Highway Administration, the relationship between state and federal welfare officials did not include much informal and friendly bargaining and negotiating on federal program standards and allotments.

The major enforcement mechanism the federal government has for ensuring compliance with its programs is threat of withholding funds. This drastic step is rarely taken, though the threat is often used. Although it would appear that the federal government could, by issuing regulations and standards and by withholding funds, make the state comply with its intentions, this is in fact difficult to do, especially in social service programs, which involve a highly discretionary judgment of how well service is being delivered. Although the federal government regulations may cause unintended side effects, such as generation of vast amounts of paperwork for reports and evaluations, it is difficult for the federal government to ensure exact compliance with its goals. As Martha Derthick has pointed out, "the attainment of federal objectives depends upon certain features of a state's political system—the prevalence of values consistent with federal actions, the presence of federal allies, the power of those allies in state politics, and the prevailing ideology of the political culture."[6]

The difference in values characteristic of high-ranking federal officials, and to a certain extent of the state's own "new management types," and those characteristic of most of the department's career personnel was often great in the 1970s. The Massachusetts system, administered by localities for so many years, still had a strong local and particularistic bias. When the state took over the welfare system in 1969, all those holding jobs in local welfare offices around the state were retained in those jobs. Very few of these workers had had formal social work training. In 1960, a study found that only 2.6 percent of public assistance caseworkers had two or more years of graduate study in social work and that half did not have a college degree.[7] Many local directors had at one time been clerical employees in local offices and, until 1965, had been permitted to become social workers by having six years of experience and by achieving a satisfactory grade on a statewide exam. Local office directors and administrators were recruited from inside the department, so that the common progression for a competent social worker was to move first to a directorship, then into the central office. This whole progression, regulated strictly by civil service, took years, so that the department's high-level administrators who came up through the ranks tended to be old.

The state takeover of welfare in 1968 allowed the commissioner some discretion in appointing department personnel, but the overall personnel makeup of the department changed very little. The turnover of social workers has always been high, generally about 33 percent each year.[8] This high turnover basically involves young social workers, however, and is not truly representative of the whole department. Of the 25 percent of the department's personnel engaged in administrative jobs, most are employees of many years who have worked their way first into the social worker ranks and gradually into administrative positions. Few have advanced professional social work credentials. Fewer still have other professional credentials such as degrees in law, administration, or management.[9]

The prevalence of career personnel who have come up the ranks of the traditional social welfare system influences the nature of the department's relationship with the constituent groups outside the department with whom it deals. In Massachusetts, many of the private social welfare agencies with which the department deals daily are, like the department itself, heavily populated with career social welfare personnel, many of whom have had careers similar to their counterparts in the government. Professional ties have historically been strong and close between private social welfare groups and the department. This relationship has been further cemented by the fact that the department has more than four hundred contracts with private agencies and spends more than $12 million annually on residential placement of its clients.[10] The result of this relationship has been that the department has had a significant group of allies outside state government who provide more support for its programs than pressure to change. Because of this, it would be misleading to argue that pressure exerted on the welfare department depends on undifferentiated "outside groups" concerned with welfare; in fact many of these groups have been among the department's staunchest allies. Much outside citizen pressure for change in recent years has come from newly created advocacy groups, such as the Office for Children (an office within the Executive Office of Human Services) and the Children's Defense Fund. These groups have tended to focus on particular parts of the welfare population (especially children) and have raised questions of legal rights and extent of coverage of services. As one staff member of the welfare department put it:

What you're dealing with in terms of citizen pressure groups is not a distinction between the people on the "inside" versus those on the "outside." Instead, you find that the traditional social work service providers on the inside and on the outside talk to each other as colleagues. They've had the same training and been the same places. The real pressure comes from the conflict between the old social service types, both in the government and outside it, and the new young advocates and the "managers." Instead of working in a mutually supportive relationship, the new advocacy groups and young professionals, lawyers and M.B.A.'s, are pushing the department very hard to pursue different goals, to initiate new programs, and to set new standards for itself. It's these people, both outside the department and inside it, who are really banging the department over the head.[11]

In addition to the concern it generated among the groups that have a special interest in welfare matters, one would have to argue that in the late 1960s and early 1970s welfare enjoyed a saliency as an issue among the general population equaled by few other issues of public policy. As one administrator of the department put it:

You simply can't discount the importance of welfare as a symbolic issue for a great many generally apolitical people. The whole business raises complex questions of rights and of obligations of members of society for each other and of who's "poor" and who's marginally making his own way. What's especially difficult about this constituency is that you can't really get ahold of it or identify in advance what will trigger it off. But it's there, it's real and it can affect what happens to the department as much as, or more than, any deliberate campaign undertaken inside or outside of the department.[12]

This widespread public concern with welfare has always been noticed and shared by the legislature, which has been extremely active and influential on welfare policy. The primary dealings of the legislature with the department, unlike its dealings with many other departments in state government, have not been on the issues of jobs in the department or constituent favors but with the broader issues of welfare spending and management of the system. Though it can help legislators with particular client services, the department has relatively few jobs or legislative favors it can bestow.[13] The issue of welfare tends instead to be treated in broader symbolic terms and often surfaces couched in terms of moral or general fiscal principles involved in running a government. As Martha Derthick has noted, "Where there is a general tendency toward moralism in public affairs (where, that is, a tendency to put moral standards into law is characteristic of the local "culture"), such a tendency is likely to be manifested in the public assistance program."[14] The Massachusetts legislature, dominated as it has been for many years by Irish Catholics and Yankee Protestants, has exhibited this tendency toward moralism on more than a few occasions.

Although the welfare issue has been debated in the legislature in the most highly emotional and symbolic terms, the Massachusetts General Court, unlike legislatures in many other states in the country, has never cut welfare benefits.[15] One analyst of welfare in Massachusetts has hypothesized that this tendency to discuss welfare as a moral issue while refusing to cut actual benefits is telling evidence of the peculiar political culture of the Massachusetts legislature. He suggests that

The legislature here is strongly ethnic, strongly Democratic, and not far removed from its immigrant background. The fact that 70 percent of the state's welfare clients are white means to these legislators that many of the recipients are not the "shiftless poor" but probably someone from their own culture down on his luck. The tradition of "taking care of your own" is extremely strong in Massachusetts. So many of the ethnic communities that are left also tend to be poor, and the chance that you'll be cutting them off is too great for many of the urban legislators to take.[16]

Thus, although the Department of Public Welfare has received a good deal of attention from the Massachusetts legislature, the legislature's response to the department has varied in intensity, specificity, and severity. Because of the complexity of the issue and because of the emotional nature of debate about it, legislators have always had a difficult time dealing with it. Consistent and predictable legislative welfare management has also been complicated because so much of the money and so many of the specifications for program content are supplied by the federal government and because the legislature has a limited capacity to appraise and anticipate federal action and intent.

The legislature is not alone in having to confront the welfare department on many levels and on many kinds of issues. In fact one could argue that the single most important thing to know about the Department of Public Welfare in understanding its management is that it has no one clearly defined task or issue with which it deals. Instead, it has responsibility for a variety of complex programs that serve different clienteles. Even the department's categorical programs are extremely diverse and have no goals that can be clearly delineated. The issues the department must confront range from the most minute and particularistic to the highly symbolic and moral. This is complicated by the fact that requirements for programs and money are set by several different governmental jurisdictions. Evaluation and regulation of the department are carried out by both the state and federal governments, and often there is no correspondence between them either in their goals or in the standards of performance they apply.

The complexity of the department's job is further complicated by the fact that its programs serve many different constituencies, each with its own particular needs and demands. These include the medically indigent, the old, the disabled, children, and other categories of the poor, as well as the general public and varieties of politicians who are deeply interested in the issue. Often providing programs for any one of these clienteles leads to charges that the department is exercising favoritism and behaving in an inequitable way.

In addition, it is extremely difficult, if not impossible, to define what high quality or successful service is for the welfare department. The department can never provide enough cash grants to eliminate any of its categories of assistance. Further, many of the social services it provides are difficult to evaluate for several reasons. Services are highly decentralized and individual offices still preserve a strong localistic tradition, so that management from the central office is difficult. In addition, many aspects of the service provided involve discretionary behavior and interaction of hundreds of social workers with thousands of clients. Finally, beyond giving a flat cash grant, it is difficult to distinguish what "providing services" means, especially when the services are as elusive as "quality day care" or "good foster care."

In short, the department has no single simple task it can easily define and work toward achieving. Its programs are varied, limited in a situation of unlimited demand, and complex both in their administration and standards for evaluation. In 1965, the National Study Service, in search of reform measures that would make the welfare system more manageable, made a detailed report. Though the report made several recommendations, one of the major conclusions of the study group was that there was no "purpose" to the welfare system. As the authors put it, after making recommendations for changes in the general laws, "Nowhere [in the general laws], however, can be found a public policy statement in respect to *purpose* of welfare programs. What is the overall purpose of these welfare services? What are the goals of the public assistance programs over and beyond providing adequate aid or assistance? Is there need for more?"[17]

The Management of the Department

Until the state takeover of welfare in 1968, the commissioner had little formal or informal authority over the welfare system. The department was highly decentralized, with three hundred and fifty local offices, one hundred of which were staffed by only one person. Though the department had the authority to monitor and to enforce standards, in fact this was very difficult, both because of the limited number of central office staff and because of the political autonomy local directors generally enjoyed.

After much heated debate, the legislature in 1967 voted to approve a state takeover of the welfare system in 1968.[18] The legislature allowed a start-up time of ten months for the department to assume control, designating July 1, 1968, as the date on which the state would be fully responsible for the functioning of all local welfare offices.

The commissioner to whom this job fell was Robert Ott, who had been appointed by John Volpe in his first term as governor and who was kept on through the Peabody and second Volpe administrations. Ott, a social worker by training, had made a career in the Massachusetts welfare system, starting as director of the Child Welfare Division of the department in 1949. He supported the state takeover and worked actively to have the plan adopted by the legislature. Unfortunately for Ott, however, both he and the legislature underestimated the difficulty of the job to be done. In 1970 Ott resigned under pressure from Acting Governor Sargent.

Ott's difficulties in getting the job done were not all due to his own weaknesses as an administrator. On the contrary, one could argue that any incumbent commissioner at the time of the takeover would have faced enormous, if not insurmontable difficulties. The apparatus of the welfare system was a shambles. There was no central payment system for welfare recipients. Local offices each functioned according to the standards of a local director, so that there were enormous discrepancies among offices in both the detail and accuracy of their records. There was no statewide list of recipients or of employees, which meant that checks for both were delayed for weeks. The addition of the responsibility for the new and enormous Medicaid program simply added to the chaos. When department supervisors attempted to evaluate the accounting system for Medicaid, they often encountered offices whose "accounts" consisted of shoeboxes filled with unpaid bills of varying ages. At the same time the department was attempting to figure out how to tackle the problem of getting its paperwork to flow smoothly, it had to negotiate new contracts for space for local offices because most of these offices had been in local facilities. The paperwork necessary for renting space once it had been located took forty weeks to work its way through the complex and cumbersome state administrative system. This meant that for long periods of time some welfare offices had no permanent geographic home. To deal with all of these problems Ott had, in addition to himself, a central office staff of fifteen.

Nor were the problems he had to face only internal. When the state assumed responsibility for welfare, it meant that the public, increasingly concerned about welfare costs, had a single agency on which to focus its attention. The National Welfare Rights Organization, with its demands for increasing benefits for welfare recipients, achieved its greatest strength in Boston in 1968 and 1969, staging several highly visible demonstrations. Politicians also began to consider welfare a salient issue and, depending on their ideological persuasion, demanded to know such things as why recipients were not being promptly paid, why the welfare rolls were increasing, or why vendors of medical services had not been reimbursed. By 1969, with a gubernatorial campaign in the offing, it became clear that welfare was a prime campaign issue. Sargent, running for election after a brief stint as acting governor, had to take action on welfare; and this action included firing Ott and bringing in from out of state a new commissioner, Steven Minter.

The timing of Minter's acceptance of the job of commissioner and of his arrival in Massachusetts was important to his becoming a strong and independent commissioner. Though he was offered the option of waiting to take the job if Sargent were elected, after conferring with the acting governor and looking at the range of the problems in the system, he agreed to come to Massachusetts immediately, with four months left in Sargent's term and no assurance that he would have a job after the election.

The arrival of Minter as the new commissioner in the August before the November election effectively deflated welfare as the election issue that might have caused Sargent to lose. There were several reasons for this. Though relatively young, Minter had made a career of public welfare, rising from a job as social worker up through the ranks to the position of director of the welfare department of Cuyahoga County, the Ohio county that administers the welfare system of Cleveland and its surrounding areas. He was familiar with both the technical issues and the politics of the welfare system and had gained administrative experience in the tough political arena of Ohio county politics. He understood and agreed with the governor's two general priorities for the welfare department, which were to work on alleviating the administrative chaos in the department while following a policy of "hang onto what you've got" in the midst of a national backlash against welfare.[19] Because of this, he was immediately able to pick up on the general issues confronting the department and speak authoritatively about them. He also had the advantage of being an extremely attractive and skillful public figure, at ease and relaxed immediately with the press and with the groups interested in welfare. Because he was a new commissioner, people were reluctant to criticize him until they had a chance to see what he stood for, and he enjoyed a period of grace that corresponded with the timing of the campaign.

The fact that he served as such an asset in the campaign, deflating an issue that had the potential to defeat Sargent, made Minter's position as commissioner strong after the election. This strength was reinforced by several other factors. Minter made it clear early that he was a team player and that as long as he and the governor agreed on priorities, he would be a model of loyalty. He agreed with the governor's liberal welfare policies and was partly responsible for formulating them in the first place, so this was not a difficult posture for him to maintain. In addition, his substantive knowledge of welfare issues was extensive, especially compared with that of the governor himself or of his chief advisors. He was able to preempt the field, especially after many of his early decisions proved to be both administratively and politically sound. Even with the appointment of a secretary of human services, nominally Minter's boss, in 1971, this tendency to look to Minter as "the expert" persisted, both because he had preceded the secretary in coming to Massachusetts and because he had already established himself as an authoritative and trusted administrator. Finally, he brought in only one staff person of his own in the early months of the administration, choosing to work with the existing staff of the welfare department. This earned him a favorable reputation with his department personnel, many of whom had feared the departure of Commissioner Ott and appointment of Minter meant there would be a significant turnover in employees.

The circumstances under which Minter took his job were fortuitous. The opportunity he had to be the new man on a tired issue provided him with momentum, both in dealing with his superiors in the governor's office and in dealing with the general public. Despite these advantages, the nature of the department and its public visibility made it subject to continuous "crises." It is a difficult department to manage. Of all of the areas in which state government deals, one could argue that the environment in which welfare policy is made is among the most complex and one that leaves the policymakers little room for discretion and choice. Unlike many other departments, where what has to be done is clearly defined, the welfare department has a large number of tasks that involved unmeasurable goals such as providing "enough" funds for medical care for the needy or promoting the welfare of the elderly or the indigent. Often the management of one of these tasks requires sets of skills entirely different from the management of another, yet the same small staff is responsible for them all. For example, understanding the extreme complexity and nuances of the Medicaid system involves skills different from those required to set up a network of community-based counseling services, yet both tasks are the responsibility of the department.

Management of the department is complicated by several other factors. Although welfare programs consume over 40 percent of the state budget, state discretion over how that money is used is extremely limited because the bulk of the monies pass through state hands directly to recipients in the form of grants or are used for programs so closely regulated by the federal government that there is no real choice about how they can be spent. This generates an additional constraint that the department must continually deal with: making certain they are not out of compliance with federal regulations, or at least not so blatantly out of compliance that they may lose federal monies. In addition, the department operates within the constraint of an outdated and clumsy civil service system. More than other state agencies the welfare department, because of the nature of its personnel, is especially heavily affected by these restrictions. For example, because the rate of turnover among social workers is so high and because the exams for social workers are given so infrequently that the civil service lists for social work positions expire, the department has to hire approximately five hundred provisional social workers each year. Often months after the department has trained and fielded these people, the test is given for social workers, with several thousand people taking the test. Of the five hundred provisionals, only 10 to 20 percent are reachable on the civil service lists and can be hired for permanent social work positions, making the turnover rate among social workers staggering and the department's loss of time and resources for training extremely high.

These constraints mean the department always has an agenda that is largely set by forces outside the department, and often outside the boundaries of state government. The problem of "running" the welfare department does not involve initiating new programs or setting an agenda but, rather, deciding in what order "crises" dictated by external forces should be handled. Sargent and Minter were confronted during Sargent's administration with a whole list of priorities all of which had some potential for crisis. What the ordering of these priorities had to be was not clear. The difficulty of the task of managing this agenda was further complicated by the fact that the items on the list never remained static.

The agenda of the department was becoming increasingly complex when Minter became commissioner in 1969. He was faced immediately with the problem of setting up a system of internal management procedures and controls for a department publicly acknowledged to be an administrative shambles. This involved setting up a complete fiscal management control system with an adequate record of recipients, vendors of welfare services, and monies and services provided. In addition, complete separation of the mechanism of determining eligibility for financial assistance from the mechanism for delivery of social services had been mandated by the federal government; and the department was losing $2.5 million each year for failure to comply.[20] In 1972, the governor added to the complexity of this task by ordering a complete reorganization of each secretariat and each department in state government, urging that the department combine its children's and family services with those of the Department of Youth Services.

On top of this, the legislature and the public called upon the department to make amends immediately for many of the problems generated by the chaos that had occurred when the state took over the welfare function. Vendors who had not been paid for their services demanded payment and a more efficient and effective way of processing bills. In addition, despite the effort underway to install management controls over the expenditure of money, as late as 1974 error occurred in approximately 50 percent of the transactions involved in providing financial assistance to recipients.[21] The federal government threatened to penalize the department financially if this rate was not lowered. Further complicating the department's agenda was the fact that the federal government in 1974 had assumed control over payments of OAA, DA, and Aid to the Blind. The department had to prepare for conversion to the new system, which involved an increment of more than $60 million in the welfare budget. In 1974, the federal government also mandated a new food stamp program to replace the old food commodities program and to cover a far broader range of people than in the past. In addition to all of these priorities, department personnel were faced with a year-long negotiation for a contract with the social workers' union, whose membership consisted of three-quarters of the state's social workers.

The commissioner's (and the governor's) choice of priorities and areas in which he wanted to involve himself in welfare was limited not only by the number of "priority" items with which the department had to deal but also by the highly political nature of the welfare issue itself. The department was visible and vulnerable because of the widespread emotional and symbolic salience of welfare. There are two distinct kinds of problems the welfare department, like other public bureaucracies susceptible to crisis management, must handle: "issues" and "incidents." The issues are those matters of policy that can be predicted, analyzed, and controlled within the normal political and administrative channels. Incidents, on the other hand, are the random, unpredictable, and often inflammatory and politically uncontrollable events that occur, which have to be responded to immediately and often with no preparation. Because of the highly emotional nature of the environment in which the welfare system operates and because of the potential for political crisis associated with it, handling incidents is a major factor in determining toward what problems the department's management resources should be directed.

Minter's administration was no exception to this rule. As he explained it: "I spend most of my time on the unpredictable events that could bring everything crashing down around our heads. Issues are important, but we share responsibility for most of them with lots of people—with the Feds, with the legislature. The incidents are more important, often involve less tangible or real things, and are viewed solely as the responsibility of the department and the governor. The management of incidents makes or breaks you."[22]

The fact that incidents in the public welfare department were so important meant that the governor and his staff often spotted the potential for crisis in the department and treated these problems as the most important ones with which the department dealt. This, combined with the fact that the department had a limited staff and limited resources, meant that taking initiatives and engaging in any form of long-range planning were not feasible.

In the Massachusetts Department of Public Welfare during Minter's tenure, these constraints on taking policy initiatives were reinforced by Minter's own preferences and administrative style. Like many other welfare administrators around the country, one of Minter's chief jobs was to maintain the level of support and service provided by the department in a political climate that favored welfare cutbacks. Partly because of his sense that this was the thing that made a good welfare administrator and partly because he considered himself better at providing steady direction of the existing system than at initiating change, Minter's style was to focus on the tasks that obviously had to be done. As Minter described his view of his job:

I'm a manager, in the traditional sense of that word. I don't consider it my job to dream up dramatic new policy initiatives. Instead, I'm a process and procedures man. Once a decision had been made about the general policy direction in which this department should move, I'll move it there. I'm responsible for how we get from point A to point B, once it's been determined where we want to be.

I'm responsible for how we get there and I'm certainly not going to ask for any supervision. If I run into a problem that should be handled by the governor or the secretary, I'll pass it to them. Otherwise, I'll keep everybody informed and do what I've set out to do and meet whatever are the most pressing priorities for the department. That leaves me or my staff with little time and few inclinations to run a think tank on welfare policy. That should be done, but it's not our job to do it.[23]

The ordering of the department's priorities seemed to fit a pattern consistent with this philosophy while Minter was commissioner. The department focused on what it absolutely had to do. The staff of the department gave primary attention to any matter that would cause the department to lose money, either because of legislative budget cuts or because of threats by the federal government to withdraw funds. Threats by the federal government were treated with varying degrees of seriousness, depending on whether the federal government's action consisted of mandating action, finding the department to be out of compliance, threatening withdrawal of funds, or threatening withdrawal of funds by a fixed date. A second tier of priorities consisted of handling various breakdowns within the system, especially those with potential for political repercussions, such as failure to pay vendors of service or an acknowledged increase in errors in computing assistance payments. Next in order of importance were questions involving provision of services that had potential to become major issues for interest groups or those with a strong stake in a particular program. For example, demands for improvement of the child welfare system or for an increase in the number and quality of social services provided by the department fell into this category. At the bottom of the list were the items that consumed departmental resources but had little potential for immediate payoff or threat, such as creation of new programs or initiation of an effort to coordinate the services or programs of welfare with those of other stage agencies.

This style of management was reinforced by and reflected in the behavior of the senior staff of the department. Though Minter brought a few more personnel into key positions, the majority of the central office staff were career welfare professionals whose first priority through the years had been operating the department "according to the rules." Minter's highest priority was to do what the department *had* to do and one of his own greatest talents was creating a strong sense of loyalty among his staff, so the senior staff's accommodation to Minter was easy. Though he brought in a handful of professionally trained "management czars" to shake up the department, essentially he respected the style and pace of the career professionals. He made few attempts to change their behavior, especially because most of the time that behavior helped him achieve his own goals.

The result was that the senior staff was highly loyal to Minter. Because of this loyalty and because of their own training, they did not press him hard to take initiatives or to change the way the department ran. This meant both that the department operated with little friction between the commissioner and his senior staff and that the incentives for dramatic proposals for change were very weak. Not only was there limited staff time to meet unlimited, constantly changing needs, but there were also strong incentives both from the commissioner and the senior staff within the organization to handle the things that everybody acknowledged "had to be done" first. As one member of the staff put it:

> The pressures not to rock the boat in this agency are overwhelming. Taking risks or proposing a new way of doing things, particularly in the face of all of the requirements that the department has to conform to, is frowned upon. It's not good to be known as someone who asks a lot of questions about why the department operates as it does. If you do, the senior staff considers you immature or they think that you don't know the ropes yet. Their view is that we've got troubles enough without having someone in the department go out of his way to give us more. It's demoralizing, especially to the younger staff in the department, but I guess that it's impossible for the department to operate any other way.[24]

Minter's sense that his job consisted of doing the things that had to be done generally enhanced his popularity and stature with groups outside the department with which he had to deal. For the governor and his staff, this quality was crucial in maintaining public support and averting crisis. Minter was not a crusader or a maverick. He was the prototype of a commissioner who was not trying to radicalize the poor but who was trying to do his job in a businesslike and fair way. His relationship with the legislature was extremely good and was cultivated carefully. Two members of the central office staff worked on legislative relations, and one of them spent almost full time tracking down problems legislators or the governor's staff had with the department. Minter also treated all legislators with friendly deference, answering all of their requests for information promptly and clearly. The result of his efforts was that though most legislators had intense and often unfavorable reactions to the policy area with which his department dealt, they liked Minter personally and generally were willing to listen to what he said.

Minter spent a great deal of time working on projecting a favorable image to groups that were potential opponents, such as the media, the legislature, and the financial community. This commitment of time was necessary because the environment in which he had to deal was so public, and public response to the department and the welfare issue was crucial in determining how much of the department's agenda he could control. That these groups generally gave him a hearing was based on Minter's own personality and efforts and in no way could be said to have been institutionalized for the department. Close relationships between the legislature and the department were not permanently cemented as they were for some of the state's other departments, such as the Department of Public Works. With few jobs or favors to offer to individual legislators and with a highly controversial public policy area to oversee, Minter had a variable relationship with the legislature that was highly dependent on his ability to woo individual senators and representatives.

The Governor and the Welfare Department

Direct involvement of the governor and his staff on matters of welfare policy has traditionally been limited in Massachusetts. Much of this tradition exists because until 1968 the state government shared responsibility for welfare with both federal and local governments. In addition, even after the state assumed control of the welfare function, there were powerful incentives for the governor to avoid associating himself with the department except when it became absolutely essential for him to intervene to ensure his political survival. The issues involved in dealing with welfare for any governor are "no win" issues—crises with no resolution, extremely complex programs with no easily measurable goals that eat up a large amount of the state budget annually, and situations that involve deeply felt and often highly polarized emotions among the general public.

In Massachusetts, these powerful incentives have reinforced the tendency of the governor's staff to shy away from any attempt to achieve control over the day-to-day workings of the department and to attempt to manage the department only when a major crisis occurs. Furthermore, the complexity of the department's goals and tasks has in many instances made policy set by the governor more difficult to enforce in the welfare department than in other state departments.

Because the department is highly visible and has potential for crisis, Sargent had to try to control it. But his ability to do this consistently and thoroughly was limited. Perhaps the best way to understand the nature of the governor's relationship with the welfare department is to look briefly at four different types of gubernatorial intervention in the department. These four examples—state assumption of control over the welfare system, introduction of the flat grant, the separation of determination of eligibility from social services, and the governor's reorganization plan of 1972—are illustrative of the kinds of attempts at managing the governor made and of the varying degrees of success with which he met.

Under pressure from the social welfare community and from many of the state's large cities and towns that were having to pay ever-increasing welfare costs, Governor John Volpe in 1967 proposed that the commonwealth assume responsibility for the administration of public assistance grants. The legislature, although it was divided on the proposal, recognized that it was dealing with an issue that could be promoted as an attempt on their part to provide a more direct line of accountability to the taxpayer for the tax dollar. This was true because one jurisdiction could be held responsible for welfare and because state assumption of payments would reduce local taxes. In addition, there were strong political pressures at work to make the General Court pass the legislation. Kevin White, the secretary of state, had just been elected mayor of Boston. John Davoren, the speaker of the House, was anxious to be named secretary of state but White, who was stepping into the job as chief executive

•

of the City of Boston, with the largest welfare population in the state, refused to yield the secretary's job until the legislature passed the state takeover bill. When the legislature did pass the bill, they did so without giving primary consideration to the relationship between the department and the governor or to the feasibility of implementing the plan. Instead, responding to political pressure and the governor's request, it passed the law, allowing ten months for the governor and the department to assume control over the welfare system.

Although Volpe had asked for the legislation, he did very little to follow up on its implementation. He retained Commissioner Ott and delegated the job of the conversion to him and the department. He and his staff made no attempt to increase their control over the system either by involving themselves in the state takeover or by providing Ott with guidance or with new resources to accomplish the absorption of a new five-thousand-person state agency. As Ott describes his relationship to the governor and to his senior staff at this time:

They said they wanted me to do the job, but they provided me with nothing more than a laying on of hands. Volpe said that he wanted to help—but no one in the governor's office understood what we were up against. We didn't just need a change of the name in the top box of the organization chart. We needed extraordinary help from every unit of government—materials, office space, speeded up checks, administrative support.

I have a tendency to go through the proper channels. But to make this department actually happen I needed the ability to go right to the top, to expedite. I couldn't do it. Volpe wouldn't lean on the people who needed to be told that I needed all the help I could get. They didn't understand what I was up against.[25]

The new "control" over the welfare department was a nominal rather than an actual attempt on the part of the governor to change welfare policy. Volpe, heavily engaged in a campaign for the vice-presidency in 1968, was not focusing on the welfare system. Sargent followed Volpe's lead when he first took office. The incentives to ignore the department were strong. The issues

involved did not seem to include any matters of crisis proportions that could affect the governor's immediate political goals.
Executing the takeover of the system consisted not of a grand
public choice that could be resolved by a forceful governor but
rather of hundreds of rather dull though complex administrative
adjustments that had to be made to make the system work. In
addition, although Sargent had supported the request for increased gubernatorial authority over the welfare department, he
had no desire to be publicly identified with the actual functioning of a creaky, poorly managed system that was coming under
increasing public scrutiny. Thus, although the law providing for
the state takeover had actually transferred control over the welfare department into the governor's hands, the control was not
seized by Volpe or immediately pursued by Sargent. Rather,
they followed a strict policy of leaving the department alone
and not attempting to interfere. The chaos resulting from the
state takeover was not addressed or dealt with in any extended
way by either governor.

A second type of gubernatorial control involves an active intervention in the department on the part of the governor to
change a policy, and subsequent success. The imposition of the
flat grant in Massachusetts is a good example both of why it became necessary for the governor to act and of why the actual
implementation of his policy occurred.

Soon after Francis Sargent became acting governor the issue
of welfare began to heat up. Welfare spending was increasing,
and public awareness of the issue was rapidly expanding. Social
workers and employees of the welfare department were dis-
gruntled because of heavy work loads, delays in receiving their
paychecks, and the chaotic state of the system. They organized
a union and began publicly to denounce the management of the
department.

In Boston, welfare rights groups were staging highly visible
and vocal demonstrations to press for increased benefits. In addition to demonstrating, the Massachusetts Welfare Rights Organization instructed recipients about how to use the grants for

"special needs" with two explicit goals in mind—to gain additional money and to throw the system into chaos. "Special
needs" grants were supplementary payments provided to recipients in addition to their basic welfare grants for such items as
food, clothing, and emergency supplies. Unlike the basic grant,
the amount and kinds of "special needs" grants were highly discretionary, depending on the judgment of the individual social
worker and on the policy of each local office. Welfare organ-
izers focused their strategy around the "special needs" grant,
urging welfare recipients both to demand more from the system
and to push so hard on the special needs provision that the entire system would have to break down.[26]

Managing the welfare system was not a high priority for Sargent when he became acting governor. Having assumed office
less than two years before the 1970 gubernatorial election, he
had had very little time to develop policies on anything and had
to concentrate most of his energies on the upcoming campaign.
It was not until late 1969, when it became clear that the management of welfare was an issue that could be crucial to his success or failure at the polls, that controlling the department
tightly enough to change its policies became important to him.

Faced with an embattled department with weak leadership,
Sargent's strategy to change the department was formulated by
members of his own staff rather than by Commissioner Ott.
Two of Sargent's policy staff members, Albert Kramer and John
Drew, were directed to study what could be done. Drew, a former social worker, spent two months in the department trying
to understand what "the problem" was. His conclusion was that
the special needs provision, which had proved to be so potent a
weapon to snipe at the welfare system for both the social
worker and the community organizer, should be replaced by a
"flat grant" of money that would be the same throughout the
state.

The senior staff of the department opposed the switch to the
flat grant. For most social workers, discretion over the use of
the special needs grant was an important mechanism of enforc-

ing compliance with their wishes on their clients. In addition to representing a change in the process with which they were used to dealing, the implementation of the flat grant also meant more work for an already severely overloaded department. Drew, along with Kramer and two liberal legislators who were involved in social welfare issues, David Liederman and Martin Linsky, formed the key group advising the governor on this matter and persuaded him that, despite the objections of the department, the change was necessary. In February of 1970, Sargent issued an administrative order calling for replacement of the special needs grant by the flat grant.

The actual implementation of the flat grant did not occur instantly or simply because the governor had spoken. The department remained reluctant to change the special needs provision or to move on it with the immediacy that the governor required. The consequence of the department's balking was that Drew, under Kramer's supervision, had to spend the next two months in the department directing the implementation of the plan himself. In this case, control of the department's behavior for the governor meant far more than issuing an order to his commissioner. The job of the governor's staff became not only to package and market the flat grant for the public as a move to "stop the run on the banks," but also to do all of the detailed planning for the administrative changes that it would involve. The governor perceived the issue to be so crucial to his electoral success that he had to take the extreme step of devoting many of the resources of his office and staff to step-by-step supervision and implementation of his policy, achieving control despite the department's reluctance.

A third example of an attempt at gubernatorial control involves the governor's operating under essentially the same constraints as the department itself in getting something done. The separation of the financial assistance function from the delivery of social services was mandated by the federal government in 1969. Both the governor and Commissioner Minter agreed that separation should be accomplished as soon as possible, especially because failure to comply was costing Massachusetts $2.5 million in federal reimbursement each year.

The governor ordered the separation and Minter and his department were in full accord with the decision, but it took until August of 1974 for a plan to be put into effect. Though it would have been extremely useful for the governor to show a decrease of $2.5 million in welfare expenditures in a budget for which he had to fight annually with the legislature on almost every penny, separation became a second-level priority on both the governor's and the welfare department's crowded and crisis-dominated agendas. Unlike the issue of the flat grant, the issue of separation was not crucial enough to the governor's survival to warrant heavy investment of his limited resources in the issue. Similarly, for Minter, though he was in full agreement with the governor's stated policy, other issues such as a centralized payment system became more crucial both to the department's smooth running and, ultimately, to the governor's credibility on the welfare issue. Although the formal statement of a policy was made, the resources necessary to carry out the policy could not be summoned up by either Minter or the governor, and separation became de facto a policy to be undertaken when other more important needs were not pressing.

A final example of a kind of gubernatorial intervention is the situation in which the governor stated a policy to which he was not willing to commit large amounts of resources and that the department did not support. The governor's proposal for reorganization of state government is a prime example of this. The state reorganization plan of 1970, which allowed Sargent to bring ten cabinet secretaries to head "superagencies" into the government, contained language urging a second "stage" of reorganization of departments by the governor in 1972. Sargent followed up on this recommendation and asked his departments to reorganize themselves within guidelines laid down by his office. He also decided to make reorganization "his issue" by submitting the budget for the 1974 fiscal year to the legislature according to the format that would be used if his proposal for reorganization were to pass. In so doing, he hoped to be credited both with accomplishing the reorganization and with saving state monies through streamlining state government.

The governor ordered that the reorganization be supervised by the various secretariats, with participation by the departments. The governor's plan for the welfare department called for dividing the department into two new departments, one an agency that would deal strictly with the financial assistance function and the other a Department of Family and Children's Services that would combine traditional welfare social services with those of the Department of Youth Services. The detailed plan for accomplishing this was to be drawn up by task forces chaired by staff of the secretariat, with participation of the senior staff of both the welfare department and the Department of Youth Services.

Though totally loyal to the governor, Minter was opposed to diverting his limited staff resources to a reorganization that appeared to provide no benefits or additional money for his department. His reluctance was strongly reinforced by his senior staff, the participants in the task forces, who felt that the reorganization was imposed from outside the welfare system by people who did not understand it. In addition they felt they should be addressing themselves to other more pressing priorities. Minter urged his staff to cooperate with the reorganization effort, but he urged them even harder to focus on such issues as separation of eligibility from services, the fiscal management project, and the food stamp program.

The result was that the reorganization proposal was put together almost entirely by the staff of the secretariat, although the governor had ordered full participation from the agencies. The governor's order of participation by the departments was not backed up by the active interest or attention of either the governor or of his own staff. In addition, the welfare department's having so many "priority" items to attend to meant that the commissioner could urge that the governor's order be enforced while devoting his staff resources to other equally pressing priorities in which he was more interested. Because the governor was not so committed to reorganization that he was willing to devote his own limited resources to managing it in the department and because all the priorities in the welfare department had to be acknowledged as important, his own order for the department to reorganize itself did not carry a great deal of weight. In fact, many of the department's employees spoke up against the plan.

The important thing for the governor was to have a reorganization plan to present to the legislature, and this he received from the secretary of human services. The content of the plan and how it fitted with ongoing departmental policy was not as important an issue and certainly not important enough to his own success as governor that he personally would intervene in the welfare department. The welfare component of the reorganization plan had little potential for escalating into a crisis issue. In this case, as in many others, the governor ordered a policy, but that order was not important enough that he felt impelled to rank it as a top priority for the department. This left Minter with the option to evaluate it himself and decide that it did not need the immediate attention that had to be given to many other pressing tasks he had to accomplish.

The extent and effectiveness of Sargent's management of the Department of Public Welfare was variable. Sargent "managed" welfare with different degrees of seriousness and achieved different kinds of successes. Even for the welfare department, which has enormous potential for crisis, his attempts to "control," that is, to change the behavior of the agency, were limited. One might argue that the variability and extent of the governor's management of the welfare department was affected by several factors. Perhaps the most important of these is the complex and undefinable nature of the welfare department's "task." The fact that welfare's goals are diffuse, undefinable, and subject to widespread and often mercurial public attention means that the extent to which either the commissioner or the governor can dictate on what issue the department's scarce resources will be focused is limited. In addition, the fact that the federal government is so heavily involved in financing the department and dictating policy guidelines means that the discretion of anyone who attempts to manage the department is limited.

The governor's ability to manage is also affected by the personality and the strength of the commissioner. In the case of Minter, the circumstances of his arrival and his early demonstrated loyalty to the governor gave him a strong base from which to deal with the governor's office. Because he always worked within any policy parameters explicitly laid down by both the governor and the secretary, he was allowed broad discretion in ordering and managing the many pressing priorities with which the department had to deal. The fact that Minter enjoyed the loyalty of his staff reinforced his discretion over the day-to-day management of the department. Minter was himself a social worker in a department filled with social workers. In addition, he regarded himself as a "process" man, a fact that bolstered his popularity in the department. As in the Department of Public Works, much of the loyalty and cooperation of the Department of Public Welfare is directed toward the commissioner and does not automatically extend to the governor. This may have important repercussions for the governor's ability to manage the department, as it did in the case of Ott and the flat grant or Minter and the reorganization.

Finally, Sargent's management of the welfare department was highly dependent on the extent to which he was able and willing to devote his own or his staff's resources to it. Because of the salience of the welfare issue and its potential importance to the governor's political survival, the governor often had to appear to deal with crises in the department himself. However, in Massachusetts in both the Volpe and Sargent administrations, there was limited staff attention given to the day-to-day management of welfare. This was true for several reasons. First, like Alan Altshuler in the Executive Office of Transportation and Construction, Minter was regarded as both the executive officer of his department and as the chief staff resource on welfare for both the governor and the secretary. Responsibility for management of the department was assumed to have been "delegated" to him. As the chief staff person, he fulfilled several crucial requirements dictated by the style of the governor's office. He consistently opted to settle disputes with other agencies or within his own agency "out of court" before they reached the level of the governor's office and therefore did not require as much of the governor's time and attention as many other agency heads. Because of his ability to limit the problems that he brought to the governor's office to those that were both serious and required a policy decision by the governor, he was liked by the staff. He allowed them to avoid the unpleasantness of bickering and was discriminating about serious issues.

The fact that the governor paid a limited amount of attention to welfare was not only a product of trust in Minter but also a function of the more general fact that Sargent used his limited staff resources for managing crises rather than for initiation of policy or for day-to-day management or control. As one observer of this in the welfare department put it:

> For the governor's office, the issue can never be running the welfare system or making policy for it. The issue has to be taking the credit or giving away the blame. Despite the fact that welfare represents 40 percent of the state budget, it consumes about 8 percent of the brainpower of the governor's staff, and that's devoted to questions of how to make the governor look good.[27]

Sargent's own tendency to avoid detailed management of the welfare department was reinforced by the nature of the issue itself. On most management issues in welfare, the governor was unable to dictate the behavior of the agency or to ensure that it act as he wanted it to act. For the governor and his staff, managing welfare seldom offered the possibility of clear rewards. There was little room for dramatic policy initiation or for intervention that would capture the public imagination. Instead, Sargent faced constraints on his ability to control the department accompanied by constant potential for crisis. This was positive incentive for him to ignore the department whenever possible.

These same characteristics of the department meant that even when he had to intervene because of a crisis, his ability to deal with the department's problems and the possibility of his appearing to manage the department successfully were limited.

Notes

1

For a good brief description of the early history of welfare in Massachusetts see the report of the National Study Service, *Meeting the Problems of People in Massachusetts, A Study of the Massachusetts Public Welfare System.*

2

All figures in the following section are taken from document *F.Y. '75 Budget: Summary of Programs and Recommendations or The Budget in English.*

3

This figure is more difficult to estimate than it might initially appear because different categories of aid are reimbursed at different levels and because some judgments of levels of reimbursement of categories are made retroactively. The 40 to 50 percent figure was supplied to me by Richard Rowland of the Public Welfare Council of Massachusetts and seems to be accurate according to several other knowledgeable welfare sources.

4

For an excellent discussion of the extent of federal influence in the Massachusetts welfare system, see Martha Derthick's *The Influence of Federal Grants.* Much of the general descriptive material in the following paragraphs is drawn from Derthick's book.

5

This analysis of federal and state relations was supplied to me largely by Dorothy Singer, assistant secretary of human services in Massachusetts and formerly in the regional office of SRS. Other knowledgeable persons in the field including Robert Ott of the Social Services Administration of HEW and Frank R. Feeley of the Department of Public Welfare have confirmed this general analysis.

6

Derthick, *The Influence of Federal Grants*, p. 214.

7

Ibid., p. 145.

8

Interview with Leon Sattenstein, assistant commissioner for administration, Department of Public Welfare.

9

Ibid. Sattenstein estimates that even in the central office fewer than 1 percent of the employees have any formal management or administrative training.

10

Interview with Steven Minter, commissioner of public welfare.

11

Interview with Jeanne Roslanowick, special assistant to the assistant commissioner for social services.

12

Interview with Charles Lidell, regional coordinator, the Department of Public Welfare.

13

Discretion over jobs and over desirable constituent favors is far more limited by federal regulations, civil service, and the nature of the service provided in the department than, for example, in the Department of Public Works.

14

Derthick, *The Influence of Federal Grants*, p. 78.

15

This was true through Sargent's tenure in office. In 1975, Michael Dukakis recommended cuts in welfare benefits in his budget and the legislature voted to decrease benefits in several categorical programs and in GR.

16

Interview with Richard Rowland, director of the Public Welfare Council of Massachusetts.

17

National Study Service, *Meeting the Problems of People in Massachusetts*, p. 7.

18

The politics of the state takeover and the action of the governor's office will be examined subsequently.

19

These priorities were articulated by both Steven Minter and John Drew, one of the governor's chief welfare advisors.

20

The $2.5 million figure was supplied to me by Richard Rowland of the Public Welfare Council of Massachusetts.

21
Figures are from an internal Department of Public Welfare study directed by Charles Lidell. It is important to note that this error rate includes several kinds of error, including errors in calculation of payments, failure to remove ineligibles from the rolls, and recipient fraud. Calculated fraud on the part of recipients accounts for only a miniscule fraction of the error rate.

22
Interview with Steven Minter.

23
Ibid.

24
Interview with a junior staff member of the department who asked to remain unnamed.

25
Interview with Robert Ott.

26
For a good discussion of the use of the special needs grant as an organizing tool for the National Welfare Rights Organization, see Larry Bailis, "Bread or Justice: Grassroots Organizing in the Welfare Rights Movement."

27
Interview with Richard Rowland.

6
**The Massachusetts
Housing Finance Agency**

The Massachusetts Housing Finance Agency, like the Department of Public Works and the Department of Public Welfare, is shown on the state organization chart as a state agency responsible to the governor. It is here that the similarities between the MHFA and these other two state agencies seem to end. Unlike the DPW and welfare, MHFA is a young agency with no "career" employees. There are only fifty-five staff members of MHFA, fewer than the number of employees in one large regional office of either welfare or public works. Even the physical facilities of MHFA set it apart. The agency is housed in the architecturally striking old Boston City Hall rather than in any of the traditional granite state office buildings. Work spaces for staff members are divided by large green plants and contemporary furniture rather than by the standard government-issue partitions found in most agencies.

A more strikingly significant difference between the large line agencies already discussed and the MHFA is the fact that the formal powers of both the governor and the legislature over MHFA are more limited than they are for other state agencies. MHFA was established as an "independent" agency, "in but not of" the state's community affairs agency. MHFA is empowered to issue bonds to raise revenue and is not dependent on the state budget for funds for staff or for operating costs. The executive director of the agency is appointed not by the governor but by a board of directors, the members of which are selected by the governor for terms of fixed length. Authorization to finance development and to issue bonds within limits set by the legislature is granted by the board, not by the governor.

It is somewhat ironic that although the governor's formal authority over MHFA is more limited than it is over other agencies, MHFA consistently behaved as Sargent wanted it to behave during his term of office. Understanding a governor's formal authority and his formal mechanisms of control over agencies provides only a limited picture of what the nature of his relationship with them is. Although Sargent had only limited

authority over MHFA and although he expended very few of his
scarce resources on "managing" the agency, it was one of the
agencies that those both inside and outside of the government
identified as "well run" and that Sargent and his supporters
pointed to as an indicator of the strength of his managerial
skills. The agency behaved as he wanted it to behave even
though he made no major effort to control it.

Despite the fact that MHFA is "in but not of" state government, Sargent's use of political and administrative resources to
affect or to remove himself from the decisions of the agency
was as important in dealing with MHFA as it was for other agencies. Similarly, many of the limitations on his "management" of
MHFA were dictated not by the structure of formal authority
but by his use of resources and by the incentives to involve himself in or to remove himself from the agency's operation.

Although MHFA is not a "line agency" of state government,
its structure is by no means unique. In Massachusetts there is a
series of "independent agencies" like MHFA, which are responsible to the chief executive because he appoints members to
their governing boards but that report directly to boards or
commissions. This category includes, in addition to MHFA,
such important arms of the state as the Massachusetts Bay
Transportation Authority, the Massachusetts Turnpike Authority, and the Massachusetts Port Authority. Governors are frequently credited with the successes and blamed for the failures
of these agencies, often with little regard for the nature of their
formal authority or the extent of their influence over them.

In order to understand the nature of the relationship between
Sargent and MHFA, it is necessary to focus on three significant
questions. First, what was MHFA's job and how did the nature
of that job affect the agency's definition of accountability? Second, how did the style and history of the management of
MHFA affect its reponsiveness to the governor and to other organizations? Finally, to what extent did gubernatorial intervention in the agency occur and what determined the frequency,

the utility, and the nature of intervention by the governor?

MHFA: Background and Description

The Massachusetts Housing Finance Agency was created by the legislature in 1968 to provide a mechanism to make low interest construction mortgage loans and permanent mortgage loans to housing developers. The legislation contained the proviso that this housing must accommodate low income persons in areas where the need for housing was great. Though the Massachusetts agency was unique in several respects, the idea that government should provide financial assistance for housing and should help make available a larger supply of dwelling units was not a new one. Since the 1930s, the federal government had provided subsidies for "housing projects" that offered housing for the poor at less than market rents. During the early 1960s, these government projects were heavily criticized on the grounds that they caused poor people to live together in ghettos rather than allowing them to be integrated into communities. At the same time, there was a great deal of public concern that the housing supply was short and that people of all income levels needed greater choice in housing. In order to meet this need and to stimulate new construction, the Federal Housing Administration and, eventually, several state housing agencies developed policies of granting low-cost loans to developers using money raised by the sale of tax-exempt bonds.

The proposal for a Massachusetts Housing Finance Agency was first made in 1965 by a Special Committee on Low Income Housing appointed by Governor Endicott Peabody and chaired by the governor's brother, Malcolm. The proposal the commission submitted was based on the model of the New York State Housing Finance Authority, an agency established in 1960 to make loans to developers of middle-income housing. The Special Commission in Massachusetts recommended that this kind of lending agency be set up but that, unlike similar agencies in other states, it should lend money only to developers who agreed to admit both tenants who paid full market rent and at least 25 percent low-income tenants.[1] The rationale for an agency of this kind was that it would use the resources of government to increase the supply of housing while avoiding the isolation of one income group from another that government-subsidized housing seemed to have encouraged.

The report of the commission included a draft bill to carry out its recommendation, and in 1966 this bill, with some minor modifications, was introduced in the legislature.[2] The House of Representatives asked for an opinion from the state's Supreme Judicial Court on the question of whether the establishment of MHFA would serve a "public purpose" by financing private construction that benefited moderate-income as well as low-income tenants. The court ruled that under the existing proposal the subsidy to low-income families was too indirect to be legitimately labeled as serving a "public purpose."[3]

In 1967, Governor John Volpe submitted an amended version of the legislation that was defeated by the legislature. Additional changes in the initial proposal were made and in 1968 the legislature passed a bill creating the agency and appropriating $300,000 as a loan to MHFA to provide financing to four sponsors of multiunit projects. In order to provide this financing, the newly created agency had to issue its first set of bond anticipation notes, and there was an additional delay in actually getting underway until the Supreme Judicial Court determined that the agency could legally issue notes under the Massachusetts Constitution. Thus, not until mid-1969 was it clear that Massachusetts could constitutionally provide low-income housing that would also provide aid to those not of low income and that MHFA could officially begin to operate.

The agency was designed with two major considerations in mind—to buffer it from politics and to provide expertise to agency personnel on the complicated questions of mortgage banking.[4] The governing board of the agency consists of seven members. Two members, the state's commissioners of the Department of Community Affairs and of the Department of

Corporations and Taxation, serve ex officio. The other five members are appointed by the governor for seven-year terms.[5] The legislation creating the agency stipulates that of the five appointees one must be experienced in mortgage banking, one trained in architecture or city and regional planning, and one experienced in real estate transactions. The governor designates the chairman.

The seven agency members make the final decision to approve or to reject the financing of all MHFA projects. They also decide on all financial questions involving the agency, including those of when and at what rates notes and bonds should be issued. In addition, the executive director of the agency and the rest of the agency staff are hired by the agency board. The staff is exempt from civil service regulation and serves at the pleasure of the board. The board members meet monthly, with various subcommittees meeting with greater frequency. The agency also has an advisory committee of fifteen members appointed by the governor. The agency is "in but not of" the state's Department of Community Affairs (DCA), which means that MHFA is technically responsible to the governor through community affairs.

The agency is funded through a variety of mechanisms, the most important of which is its sale of bonds. The agency makes mortgage and construction loans to private sponsors at below the private market rate to construct new housing or to rehabilitate housing. The funds for these loans are generated by the sale of tax exempt revenue bonds in the bond market. The legislature, though not financially obligated by the bonds, sets a limit on bond authorization, which in the 1974 fiscal year was $1.25 billion. The agency itself decides when these bonds should be issued and at what rates. The agency secures its bonds with mortgages on the housing it finances and repays the bonds from the repayment of its own mortgage loans. During the period from 1969 until the end of the 1974 fiscal year, the agency lent $536 million to eighty-two developers.[6]

In return for the low-interest loan it makes, MHFA requires that the developer put down 10 percent of the development cost and limits the developer's profits to 6 percent of the money that he puts down. In addition, MHFA imposes a series of requirements and standards that the developer must meet. Twenty-five percent of the units must be rented to low-income tenants. MHFA can refuse projects or send back for resubmission projects that do not meet its specifications. MHFA has the final authority on tenant selection and has the right to fire or replace the management department of any project.

Although MHFA imposes these requirements on developers, there are many advantages to the developer in using MHFA financing. The most overwhelming of these is that the interest rates offered by MHFA are much lower than those of the private money market. Particularly in the tight market of the 1970s this, combined with the fact that MHFA allows forty years to repay loans, made MHFA financing extremely attractive. Although the developer's profits from the project are limited by MHFA, this limitation does not take into account the profits from which developers make the greatest amount of money, which come from their sale of limited partnerships in the project to individuals as tax shelters.

MHFA covers its own operating costs and finances its staff by three mechanisms. They charge developers a fee. They also charge a small override for their notes. In addition, MHFA uses a form of arbitrage. Because the agency issues its own notes several months before developers actually need cash payments, a free cash balance often exists. This free cash generated at tax exempt interest rates is invested in short-term securities at higher rates. The profits from these investments provide the agency with its most substantial earnings.

In addition to using the revenues it receives from the sale of bonds, MHFA also subsidizes housing with federal and state housing monies. During the first several years of its existence, MHFA received interest subsidy payments from the U.S. Department of Housing and Urban Development (HUD) under Section 236 of the National Housing Act. These payments were made directly to MHFA as mortgage lender on behalf of the project owner. The benefits of this subsidy were passed on to eligible tenants in the form of lower rent. MHFA projects were also eligible for federal leased housing programs in which local public housing authorities used federal money to lease units in a project from the owner and then to sublet to low-income tenants selected by the authority.

In January of 1973, HUD issued a moratorium on processing all applications for assistance, which caused federal housing assistance for additional production to become almost nonexistent. This meant that MHFA had to rely increasingly on state monies for rental assistance and subsidies for new developments. In the early days of MHFA, the agency members and the staff planned not to use the state's small subsidy program at all but instead to rely completely on their own revenues and on federal money.[7] When federal monies began to dry up, MHFA was forced increasingly to seek assistance from two of the state's housing programs and to urge that they be increased. The state has an interest subsidy program (the so-called "13-A" program) that authorizes MHFA to provide rent subsidies to projects and that is funded by annual appropriation by the legislature. In the 1974 fiscal year this $1 million program provided moderate income subsidies for a thousand units of MHFA housing. In addition, the state has a leased housing program that is administered by the Department of Community Affairs. Of the total leased housing program budget of $5 million in 1974, MHFA projects received the majority of funds, although DCA was free to use the money for other leased housing projects. In many cases, MHFA piggybacked the two state subsidy programs, using the interest subsidy program to reduce rents to moderate income level and then using the state leasing program to subsidize the difference between moderate-income and low-income rents.

The staff of the agency handles the day-to-day transactions, including financial analysis, design and oversight of construction, and management of the projects. The staff is made up largely of individuals with highly developed expertise in one of these areas. Although during the Sargent administration the staff was relatively young, with most of the senior officials in their early forties and the rest of the staff in their early thirties, most had had considerable experience as private developers, mortgage bankers, or as housing managers. The majority of the staff of fifty-five had worked in no other public sector job. There were several reasons for this. First, training in the specialized fields of mortgage banking and real estate development required by MHFA is more commonly done in the private sector than in general purpose government housing or redevelopment agencies. In addition, because MHFA deals primarily with the private sector, experience and credibility with the private sector have always been highly valued by agency personnel.

The turnover rate of employees at MHFA was unusually low from 1969 until 1974. Although new staff was hired after the agency started in 1969, most of these individuals came into the agency to fill new positions rather than vacancies. Unlike salaries in other government agencies, MHFA salaries were competitive with those in the private sector, with the executive director's salary at $45,000 in 1974 and several senior positions in the $30,000 per year bracket. In addition, most of the staff members were the first incumbents in their jobs, which meant that they had considerable freedom to shape their jobs to suit their own inclinations, preferences, and talents.

Finally, the agency was considered a desirable place to be during the Sargent administration because of a set of intangible features that were reflected in the overall operating style of the agency and that seemed attractive to young, experienced professionals. Although after a struggle of several weeks the agency staff was able to provide an organization chart requested by the state auditor, the agency had little sense of hierarchy. Almost all decisions were made in collegium and were not accepted until there was a consensus. Important decisions on construction and maintenance of projects were made in large meetings with all staff members invited to participate. Because of the expertise of the staff, although the agency board members were technically the executive authority of the agency, they were in fact heavily dependent on the staff and on the executive director. Though the agency members had the power to appoint the staff, often it was the staff that was responsible for recommending to the governor the list of names from which he selected agency members. The staff was also responsible for generating names of people to serve as members of the advisory committee. The advisory committee in turn made recommendations of names to the governor to fill slots on both the advisory board and the agency board. Traditionally the governor named to the agency those the advisory board suggested. This meant the staff of the agency was often heavily involved in the selection of the persons to whom MHFA reported. Because both the executive director and the staff had had experience in the field, knew almost everyone in the profession, and worked at their jobs full time, their recommendations and suggestions were highly regarded. The executive director and some members of the staff came to every board meeting and presented back-up material for all the decisions on which the agency members had to vote. They also responded to questions. The agency members seldom voted against a staff recommendation, although occasionally they raised a question that required further study by the staff.

Management of the Agency

During the Sargent administration MHFA was widely acclaimed as being one of the truly successful agencies of state government. To understand why it enjoyed such a good reputation, one must analyze the nature of the agency's task and the style of management the agency adopted to accomplish its goals.

MHFA's job is to lend money, much as a commercial bank does. The housing it finances accomplishes a social goal, providing good housing for mixed income tenants. However, the primary measure of MHFA's success is far more clear cut than that of most other government agencies. The agency's success hinges on whether it can sell bonds and provide capital for housing as well as private sector institutions can.[8] The more successful the agency is at financing sound, rentable housing, the better off its bondholders, developers, and tenants are. The social purpose of providing good housing often rides in on the back of satisfying the private market. For example, the MHFA staff has always been able to argue that without high-quality construction and without amenities such as swimming pools and recreation centers, their developments would not be rented by those who pay market rents. The agency, which would be barraged with criticism for providing such unnecessary luxuries in traditional public housing, is therefore able to provide high-quality housing to low-income tenants while remaining relatively free from the constraining influence of public reaction.

The market appeals to the self-serving interests of everyone involved. Developers make profits. Individual investors can find highly satisfactory tax shelters. Bondholders receive tax-free interest. The housing stock is increased, with all levels of income groups mixed in high-quality housing. As William White, the executive director of MHFA put it:

> In this business I'm beginning to believe that that government which governs best governs least. If you start from the simple fact that there are a lot of people in this country who deserve a fair crack at good housing and say you want to do something about it, you have to do more than just say that. You have to offer incentives to make people want to participate—and there are no incentives like letting people make some money. We provide good housing and everybody makes money. They should all be happy.[9]

For all practical purposes, one could say that during the Sargent administration the agency had only one executive director, William White. Although early in 1969 the agency board hired David Martin, a development officer at Yale University, to be the agency's first director, he was dismissed by the agency after six months and White, the agency's popular mortgage expert, took over. Both because of the strength of his own personality and because he was the only executive director of a relatively new agency, White had a strong impact on the operating style and orientation of the agency. Like most of the staff he hired,

White had been involved in private development and in real estate before coming to MHFA. Although he came to the agency because of the important social purpose that it served, his goal was to make the agency a professional one that would be respected by professionals like himself in the private market.[10] This sense of having a job to do that required technical expertise, political astuteness, and commitment was the dominant norm of the agency.

White consistently and consciously managed the agency in a way to reinforce this norm. He hired very few "generalists" or floating trouble shooters. As one staff member put it:

General academic credentials almost work against you here. We're not in business to display an impressive set of resumes. People who've specialized in nothing can't help us with the hard questions of how large our capital reserve account should be or how to shape up the management department of one of our projects. Our purpose, unlike that of a lot of other government agencies, isn't even to spend our time taking the political temperature. We're here to get housing built.[11]

White further reinforced the sense of the importance of highly developed expertise by deliberately limiting the size of the staff. Although he had the resources to hire many additional staff people and he was urged to do so by the board, he set an absolute limit of sixty on the size of the staff. He describes this limit as crucial to his ability to run the agency:

If you let the staff get any bigger than it is now, it'll become a bureaucracy, something that no one has control of. Now I know what everybody's doing without having to have some formal set of rules saying that this one reports to that one. It's important to keep it small because everyone can deal with everybody else and have a sense that what we value here is quality, not just numbers. You simply would lose the sense of the quality, commitment, and skill of everybody concerned if the place had a couple of hundred people.[12]

White not only limited the size of the MHFA staff; he also limited the nature of the agency's task to the agency's original purpose of financing housing. From the time the agency began operation, board members, citizen housing groups, and legislators suggested that the agency be involved in development as well as in financing like the Urban Development Corporation in New York. Undertaking this function almost certainly would have involved giving the agency the power of eminent domain and the power to initiate projects of its own. Unlike many other agencies for which expansion of power and scope becomes an end in itself,[13] MHFA's staff resisted taking on these new powers. White frequently and strongly expressed his opposition to MHFA's assuming the development function:

You can only do so many things well. If we diffuse our energies too much or grow too large, we'll only be able to do a mediocre job. We want to increase the supply of housing. We're doing that well. We don't need the power of eminent domain. It would make us into a different kind of agency. We can't become a cesspool of projects that everybody gives to us because we've done one thing very well. If we did, we'd lose our effectiveness.[14]

White used this same argument to fend off suggestions from the governor's office that new agencies and new functions be given to MHFA because of the agency's reputation for doing things well.

The agency's management style reflects the nature of the agency's task, the staff's background, and White's own personal method of management. The notion that "bureaucracy is bad" had always been pervasive throughout the agency and many of the usual trappings of government bureaucracies were flamboyantly avoided. During the Sargent administration, important decisions were made in large staff meetings, with vigorous discussion by all members of the staff that continued until a consensus was reached. As one of the agency board members described the operation of the staff: "It's certainly not like any traditional decision-making process that I've seen before. It might be better described as a 'happening.' "[15]

Although MHFA is a government agency, an impersonal style of operating, devoid of any flair or innovativeness, has always been completely inimical to the MHFA staff; and a good deal of ingenuity has been directed at avoiding the pitfalls of being "just another agency." When the state auditor criticized MHFA for spending too much money for use of state automobiles, the agency staff chose the less costly route of leasing cars. The fact that this included leasing a BMW for the director further outraged the auditor and was a source of some satisfaction to agency personnel.

Although much of the rhetoric of the director and the staff was directed against the dangers of "bureaucratization," much of the agency's success during the Sargent administration was the result of using the most important weapon of a classic bureaucracy, namely, the application of fixed rules to specific situations. Undeviating application of rules was particularly crucial in two areas that heavily influenced the agency's operating style. The first of these involved the regulation of developers. One of the things that differentiated MHFA from other agencies during the Sargent administration was the extremely unusual way it staged its regulatory process. Its personnel strongly encouraged innovation and entrepreneurship among developers while they regulated heavily the quality and nature of the final product its developers produced. The agency staff had a sense of social purpose and encouraged development of high-risk housing that the private market might avoid. This helped stimulate the development of a group of designers, developers, and architects who were interested in the innovative and high-quality kinds of housing MHFA tended to reward. This development occurred among the MHFA staff as well as among outside professionals. During the Sargent administration the staff was made up of the same kinds of people who probably would have been involved in MHFA projects had they not been part of the agency. MHFA personnel had a reputation within the industry for responding favorably to innovative, high-quality design and packaging. Thus the agency was seldom criticized as a "typical," "dull," "unimaginative," or "unresponsive" bureaucracy by developers who were used to dealing with more conservative private or government financial institutions.

Although MHFA often rejected proposals by developers in the

early stages of negotiations with them, it generally did so because their quality was not high enough rather than because they were too radical or because they departed from convention. It was not in the design stage, but after the projects were under construction that MHFA regulated the developers with volumes of rules. These were designed to ensure that the completed housing was and would remain of the quality agency personnel wanted. As one of the staff members of the agency put it:

Toward the end of the process, we tie developers up in knots. We let them be innovative when they should be innovative. But we need to guarantee a good product, which means that we have to be prepared to make sure that they manage the project properly and that they don't in effect take the money and run. We have to make certain that we have recourse to prevent this from happening, and our answer has been to have a helluva lot of rules which serve a very positive and important function.[16]

As a result of this use of rules, MHFA was a highly unusual kind of agency. It served a regulatory function; but unlike many regulatory agencies that apply rules with no discrimination among clients, it also encouraged and provided support for innovation and entrepreneurship in the design and start-up phases of development.

A second "bureaucratic" technique that was important in the management of MHFA during the Sargent administration was White's use of the equal application of rules as protection from those who wished the agency to provide them with special favors. White's decision early in his tenure as director to make no exceptions to the rules the agency laid down for selection of sites and of developers and for establishing the order in which projects were to be funded protected the agency from one of the areas with greatest potential for scandal that the agency faced. When he first assumed his office, White delivered an ultimatum to developers, the governor's office, and legislators that he would not hire anyone in his agency who did not have the technical qualifications to handle the jobs the agency had to do. Although "bureaucracy" was one of the loudly proclaimed enemies of the agency, the director and the staff used one of the strongest weapons of a bureaucracy, unbending application of rules, to protect themselves from pressure that could have led the agency into a scandal or could have diverted it from its task.

This universal application of rules had a marked effect on the nature of the demands that various constituents placed on the agency. After initial demands from all comers for special favors were refused, the enforcement of rules equally in all situations became a kind of insurance policy for the agency's constituents that nobody was receiving special favors. As White described it:

> That initial decision not to bend was hard to enforce. But it turned out to be a smart move in the long run. Once the word got around that the rules were the rules, nobody felt that anyone was getting special treatment.
>
> This completely changed the nature of the kind of political pressure on us. When legislators or the governor's office call about a constituent favor or a job, they don't care as much about our being unable to produce it for them as they do about having something to report back to their constituents about how the rules work or where they are on a list that allows no exceptions. All they need is some answers.[17]

The way MHFA personnel defined the agency's task and the way the agency set about carrying it out influenced both the makeup and the expectations of MHFA's constituency. MHFA limited its task to providing money for housing, much as a bank would. Because it did not undertake a variety of social functions in addition to that of financing housing for low-income individuals and families, its primary dealings with groups outside government were with private investors and developers. Although the results of MHFA action were highly visible to community groups and citizens, the actual mortgaging function they performed was extremely complicated and technical in nature and was not widely understood by a large segment of the population. In instances where the general public was involved with a specific project, it was the developer and not MHFA staff who became highly visible. Because of the nature of MHFA's mandate to operate as a financial institution, it was not expected to serve a variety of social goals.

MHFA's most important constituents were a highly specialized group made up of developers, investors, bond holders, and bankers whose foremost concern was with how MHFA met the test of the private market and with how well MHFA functioned as a business. It was in the interest of developers and bondholders alike to help MHFA pressure the legislature and the governor for large subsidies and for high bonding authorization. The major demand of MHFA's private marker constituents was that MHFA provide low-cost financing that produced profits for all concerned. As long as it did this, those firms in the private market that dealt with MHFA could be counted upon to be vocal and strong proponents of the agency before the legislature and the governor.

The members of the agency board in some sense symbolized this particular private market constituency and often were among the agency's strongest boosters. During the Sargent administration the board was made up primarily of leading members of the business community that MHFA serves. Their ties to the private sector were strong and based on shared expertise; as a result they were able to mobilize the investment and banking communities to support MHFA efforts. At the same time, because of their prestige and expertise, they served as a shield for the MHFA staff and fended off interference by other government agencies on the grounds that interference would be economically unsound or would damage the private market in which they were the acknowledged experts.

Because of the technical nature of the agency and the fact that the agency built thousands of housing units without showing noticeable favor to any special interests, MHFA was popular in the legislature during the Sargent years. The issue with which MHFA deals, providing housing, had a good deal of political currency in the late 1960s and early 1970s in Massachusetts and across the country. Because MHFA built housing and did it according to widely publicized and equally applied standards, the Massachusetts legislature approved most of MHFA's requests, making itself look good in the process. As one observer put it: "Providing housing through use of MHFA funds is a 'motherhood issue.' People get nice housing and the agency is clean and scandal free. How can you be against it?"[18] Questions about how the financing of mortgages is done are complicated and were beyond the ken of most legislators. During the Sargent administration, MHFA had one legislative relations specialist who kept legislators informed about MHFA's progress and monitored all housing proposals in the legislature that affected MHFA. The agency also provided information on tenant selection and development policies to legislators, along with a precise interpretation of the rules governing MHFA projects. Legislators were treated courteously and even-handedly, and as a result the agency enjoyed a widespread popularity.

Perhaps more interesting than looking at MHFA's supporters is analyzing its lack of opposition. Unlike other government agencies that provide housing to low-income populations, MHFA was seldom criticized for bringing "undesirable" tenants into residential neighborhoods. This was true for several reasons. First, MHFA housing was successful in the market. It had proved desirable and well-designed enough to attract tenants at market rents even though they lived in the same facilities as low-income families. Second, during the entire Sargent term there were no indicators that in well-managed buildings low-income tenants were less desirable neighbors than anyone else or that those who lived in MHFA buildings perceived them as such.[19] Third, MHFA engaged in an aggressive public relations campaign that consisted of showing off the projects they financed to legislators, politicians, and critics of the agency. Finally, the pressure from communities on even the most highly controversial projects with which they dealt was always directed first at developers, not at MHFA. MHFA provided financing and did not forcibly put any housing in place. Thus they seldom were in the position of being held responsible for anything but visible successes.

The Governor and MHFA

Like the personnel of the Department of Public Works and the Department of Public Welfare, the MHFA staff had infrequent contact with the governor's staff or with Sargent. MHFA's relationship to the governor's office differed significantly from these other two agencies, however, because the governor's staff did not claim they ever tried to manage MHFA in order to change its behavior. This was true for two reasons. First, the governor's formal authority over MHFA was more limited than his authority over the line agencies. Though this was an important rationale for not expending scarce resources on the agency, a second factor was even more important. The agency generated no crises. Instead it functioned successfully. There were three components to its success. First, by the end of the Sargent administration it had financed more than thirty-thousand housing units. Much of this housing was in place and visible by the time of the 1974 election. Second, the agency did not get into any trouble. There were no major foreclosures or scandals that might have led the public or the governor to notice what it was doing. Finally, partly as a result of these first two factors and partly because of an aggressive attempt on the part of the agency to cultivate a good public image, the agency was perceived as successful. This perception was shared by government officials and the public, though few people understood clearly how the agency actually functioned or what it did. The significant thing about the relationship between the agency and the governor was not that he had limited formal powers over the agency but that the agency performed satisfactorily enough that he never had to use his resources in order to try to change the agency's behavior.

Sargent's personal involvement with White or his staff was

limited and focused on discussions of the agency's accomplishments.[20] The responsibility for the agency shifted among members of the governor's policy staff during the years after MHFA was created. The most intensive attention given to the agency by the governor's office was at the time of its formation. Between the beginning of Sargent's term and the beginning of 1974, the responsibility for all dealings with the agency was delegated by the policy staff to the Executive Office of Commerce and Development, the secretariat through which the agency reported. Although the governor's staff responded to requests from MHFA for the governor's support on such issues as a protest to HUD over cuts in housing subsidies or on other federal policies, until 1974 the governor's staff did not initiate any dealings with MHFA. In the summer of 1974, two members of the governor's staff met with staff members of MHFA to propose that MHFA work with the governor's office to design an economic development program that would include monies for additional housing subsidies and a new industrial development finance authority. Beyond this project, the contact between the governor's staff and MHFA was minimal although White regularly informed the governor's office what he was accomplishing.

The most significant formal control the governor has over MHFA is the authority to name the members and head of the agency board. The screening for these appointments in both the Volpe and the Sargent administrations was done by the governor's Office of State Service, the personnel and patronage office of the executive staff. Although naming personal loyalists to this board was probably the most obvious way the governor could have influenced the board's policy, Sargent and his policy staff were never involved in the actual selection of board members.[21] Instead, the Office of State Service selected one board member from among three names submitted by the MHFA's advisory committee. Until 1974, the Office of State Service, which handled all but the most controversial of the twenty-five hundred board and commission appointments, automatically took the top recommendation of the advisory committee without interviewing the candidate. In 1974 the Office of State Service instituted a policy of interviewing leading candidates for important boards, and therefore interviewed candidates for a vacancy on the MHFA board. Their selections continued to coincide with the recommendations of the advisory committee. The governor and his chief policy staff neither interviewed the candidates nor attempted to determine what their stands on MHFA policies were or the extent of their loyalty to the governor. Unlike many political executives, Sargent was not personally involved in board appointments nor did he make loyalty to him the prime criterion for appointments to boards that ran agencies.

The most frequent point of contact between MHFA and the executive branch was the Department of Community Affairs (DCA), a line agency that was part of the Executive Office of Commerce and Development. During the Sargent administration, the nature of the relationship between MHFA and DCA was an unusual one. Officially, MHFA is "in but not of" DCA, which means that DCA is a conduit for MHFA business with the executive without controlling its budget or its policies. During the Sargent administration the two agencies were often competitors for the same housing assistance money. The two agencies also competed as sources of expertise on housing. Although DCA was the governor's own line agency to deal with housing matters, MHFA had a far larger and more experienced staff than DCA. In addition DCA had always been relatively weak and caught up in a good deal of administrative and political conflict.

The potential for the commissioner of DCA to exercise control over MHFA was considerable. The state rental assistance program and the state housing subsidy program were administered by DCA. Because of the nature of the grant, DCA had little discretion over how the interest subsidy money was used, but it did have considerable choice over how to distribute the rent supplement monies. MHFA always received most of this money, largely because it committed projects to construction under the assumption that the rent subsidies would be available and because it did this before DCA was able to find a use for the money elsewhere. Until 1974, the adroitness of MHFA's staff at committing these funds made it a virtual certainty that a large proportion of state dollars allocated to rent supplements would go to MHFA projects. In fact, the first administrator of the rent subsidy program in DCA had been on MHFA's payroll and "on loan" to DCA to set up the program.

After 1974, the assumption that rent supplement monies would go to MHFA changed. DCA began to raise questions about MHFA policies and about MHFA's use of state housing dollars. In 1973, after a series of political incidents involving DCA and after several commissioners had been hired and fired in rapid succession, the governor appointed Lewis Crampton to be head of DCA and gave him several more staff positions than previous commissioners had had. At the same time, the major focus of DCA changed from regulation of public housing and urban renewal to housing built by private or limited-profit enterprises with government subsidies. DCA began to have plans of its own for granting rent supplement money to local housing authorities and to groups that would focus on putting the existing housing supply to new uses.[22] Crampton was not anxious to hand over automatically to MHFA all of the funds over which he had discretionary control.

Tension between the two agencies was based not only on competition for funds but also on competition over the right to set certain aspects of housing policy. Although MHFA did finance the rehabilitation of some housing, most of its projects were newly constructed. The DCA staff had a philosophy that favored emphasis on rehabilitation of existing housing. In addition, DCA's analysis of where housing needs were greatest differed substantially from the analysis of MHFA staff members. DCA personnel were also critical of MHFA because a majority of the units it constructed were one- or two-bedroom units, not suited to accommodating poor large families who needed more space. The inclination of the MHFA staff was to construct as much high-quality housing as possible as soon as possible; the bias of the DCA top staff, made up largely of planners, was to look at the long-run implications of housing decisions. Most important of all, as a general purpose government agency, DCA had a mandate to deal with the complex range of social and political problems of communities. It therefore focused on the interaction of a series of complicated variables. MHFA, on the other hand, had a more limited, more clear-cut task: to finance housing of the highest quality that would be financially successful in the private market.

As a result of this competition, the potential for conflict between the two agencies and for the DCA commissioner to attempt to exercise control over MHFA was high. The commissioner had several weapons at his disposal in addition to allocation of the rent supplement program. Part of his job was to submit and approve all environmental impact statements for MHFA-financed projects. He also was the official conduit for any MHFA requests to the legislature and to the governor's office. Finally, he was an ex officio member of the MHFA board.

Although he had several potential mechanisms for control of MHFA, the commissioner never took on the agency on any issues except approval of each MHFA request for rent supplements. There were several reasons for this. First, and most important, neither the governor nor his staff ever tried to exert control over MHFA through the commissioner. Second, although DCA increased its staff, that staff could not begin to compete in size or skill with that of MHFA and therefore could not corner the market on providing advice on housing policy for the governor. Third, MHFA was more visible in its successes than DCA was, so it enjoyed the approval of both the governor and the legislature. Even if the governor had instructed DCA to "take on" MHFA, it is clear that such an action would have met with overwhelming opposition both in the legislature and among the governor's staff.

The only other part of the executive branch besides DCA that attempted to exercise any control over MHFA was the Office of Fiscal Affairs of the Executive Office of Administration and Finance. The budgeting arm of any executive office has the potential to be one of the strongest focuses of a governor's use of informal mechanisms of control over agencies. Although in Massachusetts the governor does not control the operating funds or bond revenues of MHFA, all state subsidies to housing are part of his budget. Because during the Sargent administration the amount of federal money for housing assistance decreased dramatically, MHFA became increasingly dependent on state money to provide assistance to the 25 percent of its tenants who by law had to be in the low-income category. The potential effect of any regulation by the executive office through use of the budget process became increasingly serious.

Although there was potential for the governor's office to exert some control over MHFA through administration and finance, in fact there was no effective attempt to control MHFA through the budgetary apparatus during the Sargent administration. This was largely because Sargent himself felt no need to attempt to exert control over MHFA. But there were also several other reasons for this that are significant because of what they explain both about the style of the Sargent administration and about the strengths of MHFA. First, the key policy advisors of the Sargent administration had neither the training nor the inclination to use the budgetary process to gain administrative control. Although the Fiscal Affairs Division of the Executive Office of Administration and Finance technically had responsibility for preparation and analysis of the budget, the personnel were not among the inner circle of the governor's advisors and they did not have easy access to the governor himself.

This fact had a significant impact on the relationship between MHFA and the Fiscal Affairs Division of administration and finance. In the 1974 fiscal year, MHFA informally requested and received a $2 million interest subsidy from the legislature without first going through the Fiscal Affairs Division for approval of its request. As a result, the head of fiscal affairs ordered that the housing subsidy programs be more closely scrutinized by his own staff. Their attention was focused particularly on DCA's request for an additional $2 million in rental assistance, half of which was to go to MHFA. Although the appropriation had already been passed by the legislature, fiscal affairs threatened to use its power to hold up the allotment of funds in order to achieve some control over DCA and MHFA spending. This effort was not successful, largely because of DCA and MHFA pleas to the governor's office and threats to take their case to the legislature.

The disagreement between fiscal affairs and MHFA was especially important because of what it symbolized about the relationship between the two agencies and about their relationship to the governor's office. As Bob Eskind, the chief budget analyst involved in the controversy, admitted, the move was in part an attempt to chastise MHFA for not showing deference to administration and finance:

They don't pay attention to the executive budgeting process. They're sloppy because their contacts with the legislature are so good and their image is so favorable. They don't have a sense of the overall size of the budget or of the limits we have to live with. What we have to be able to do is balance housing off against other equally pressing priorities. They already have an extremely heavy subsidy in the form of tax-free bonds and interest subsidies. Maybe additional state monies that they want should go elsewhere.[23]

Although the Fiscal Affairs Division committed itself to monitoring MHFA more closely, it was unable to exercise significant control over MHFA for several reasons. First, MHFA was a highly popular agency, both with the governor and with the legislature. The Fiscal Affairs Division, on the other hand, was not close to the governor's policy staff and had outraged both other agencies and the legislature when it attempted to control their expenditures and to balance overall policy priorities. Second, fiscal affairs had only one budget analyst covering housing. He also had responsibility for programs in mental health, public health, and youth services. MHFA, on the other hand, had a large staff of experts in the complicated housing finance field.

This expertise was reinforced by the prestige and skill of a board appointed by the governor. Finally, and perhaps most important, the governor's staff was most inclined to take issue with an agency when there was a crisis; by their definition fiscal planning and control of single agencies were rarely crises.

Thus, although there were several potential points in DCA and in the budgetary process at which the governor could have intervened to increase his control over MHFA, Francis Sargent did not find it necessary to do so. He was not deeply involved in MHFA board appointments. The two instances in which he dealt with MHFA were not attempts to control the agency but rather to bring closer the association of his name with the agency's good reputation. Sargent's 1974 proposal of an economic development package was an election year response to strong criticism by the business community and by opponents of his handling of the state's economic situation. The decision by his staff to tie MHFA into the proposal was made both because of the MHFA staff's reputation for high-quality work and because of the agency's general popularity with the business and economic community.[24]

For similar reasons, the other major dealings between the governor's staff and MHFA involved the governor's staff's proposal that MHFA take on new functions. These initiatives included proposals that MHFA help set up an industrial finance authority and that the legislation for MHFA be expanded to include in its mandate responsibility for development. It was because of White's resistance to enlarging the agency that MHFA did not become more powerful and assume more functions.

Although Sargent did not consider it necessary to attempt to control MHFA, there is nothing inherent in the governor's office or in the structure of MHFA that dictated the nature of this relationship remain constant over time. The fact that the agency was more independent from formal control than many line agencies did not mean that a governor would never *want* to control it. One of the primary thorns in Sargent's side was the Massachusetts Port Authority, similar in structure to MHFA, with a board appointed by the governor. That Sargent never made a public effort to control Massport was due more to his belief that he would lose than to his lack of interest.

One could argue that there are several situations in which Sargent might have found it necessary to take some action to try to control an agency like MHFA to ensure that he was not placed in political jeopardy by it. If the agency had been involved in a scandal or in a major market disaster, he would have had to intervene. In both these cases, the interest of the board of the agency in keeping the agency in a sound financial position probably would have meant that the board itself would have had to take action to correct the situation and to bring the agency under control.

A second and more difficult situation in which Sargent or any governor might have had to intervene would have occurred if the agency were doing nothing and this fact became publicly known. Had this happened, Sargent would have had to fall back on the informal means of control available to him. These might have included using the powers of DCA and of administration and finance to regulate the agency, asking publicly for resignations of board members or the executive director, attempting to rally citizen support against the agency, or putting his own staff into the agency. These actions, and the others like them that the governor would be able to take, all would involve an element of risk.

The third kind of situation that might have prompted Sargent to intervene in MHFA affairs could have arisen if Sargent had formulated a clear, long-term housing policy that he wanted to carry out or if he had feared that the executive director or the board were seizing control of an area of housing policy in which he wanted a voice. In attempting to manage this situation, like the case in which the agency was not doing enough, the governor would have had to compete with other constituents for control over the agency; and his effectiveness at managing would have depended on his own and his staff's ability to convert political resources into mechanisms of control. This situation did not occur, however, because Sargent had no policy on housing more detailed or more clearly formulated than approving what MHFA was already doing.

During Sargent's term MHFA was a good example of an agency to which the governor had to devote very few scarce resources but that performed "well." The definition of executive control includes "changing the behavior of an agency at a cost of scarce resources." Sargent did not attempt to control the agency because he had no desire to change the nature of the agency's performance. MHFA's principal task, lending money to build housing, was simple to define but required highly skilled expertise to execute. Actual administration of the agency involved deciding complex fiscal questions that were not overtly political. In addtion, pondering questions of long-term planning for MHFA and for housing in general were a luxury that a crisis-oriented governor and his staff thought they could not allow themselves. Instead, if they had any dealings with the agency, it was likely to be to find out what a good job the agency was doing and to reinforce their impression that the agency was operating as a political credit to the governor. The governor had little need to change the performance of the agency because he reaped the benefits of its performance without having to devote his resources to it. Housing was built in *his* administration by *his* agency but without his expending resources of staff time or political clout.

The relationship between Francis Sargent and MHFA was in some ways unique because of the characters involved, but it can also be seen as representative of a particular type of gubernatorial management. The agency had an easily isolated task that it performed well. The director of the agency was strong and his management style was well suited to the task and desires of the agency's constituency. From the governor's perspective the agency did what it was supposed to do without his intervention, and he therefore made no attempt to change its behavior.

Notes

1

Final Report of the Special Commission on Low Income Housing.

2

Most of the information on the early history of MHFA is drawn from two sources: Massachusetts Housing Finance Agency "First Annual Report" and the files of the Citizens Housing and Planning Association.

3

Opinion of the justices of the Supreme Judicial Court to the House of Representatives, 351 Mass. 716 (1966).

4

Interview with John Ryan, a member of the first MHFA board and one of the architects of the MHFA legislation.

5

Three of the initial appointments were made for three-, five-, and six-year terms respectively so that the entire board would never be inexperienced and so that one governor would not make all of the board appointments.

6

Wall Street Journal, June 25, 1974. The fiscal information that follows comes from three sources: the *Journal* article, the MHFA annual reports, and interviews with MHFA staff.

7

Interview with William White, executive director of MHFA.

8

One illustration of the importance of MHFA's ability to sell bonds as a measure of its success was the wave of questions and criticisms directed at the agency in late 1975. Because of the general instability of the municipal bond market, there was some question about whether MHFA would be able to sell its bonds at all. When MHFA bonds were offered in early 1976, they were sold at a record rate of interest, and there was a great deal of speculation in government and in the financial community about MHFA's ability to survive.

9

Interview with William White.

10

Ibid.

11

Interview with Matthew Hobbs, assistant to William White. Hobbs was the closest to being an exception to the rule of not hiring generalists on the staff. He covered a variety of issues and had a degree in urban planning.

12

Interview with William White.

13

See Matthew Holden, "Imperialism in Bureaucracy."

14

Interview with William White.

15

Interview with Hope Funkhauser, member of the MHFA board.

16

Interview with Steven Ryoff, head of the rental division of MHFA.

17

Interview with William White.

18

Interview with Lewis Crampton, Commission of Community Affairs, August 7, 1974.

19

Citizens Housing and Planning Association of Metropolitan Boston, *All In Together*.

20

Interview with William White.

21

This is based on interviews with Ricki Moriarity, assistant to the director of the Governor's Office of State Service and with Tom Glynn of Sargent's staff.

22

The material in the following paragraphs is based on interviews with Joel Kershner, director of the state subsidy program in DCA; Steven Ryoff, formerly the director of this division; and Lewis Crampton, commissioner of DCA.

23

Interview with Bob Eskind.

24

Interview with Tom Glynn.

7

**The Department
of Mental Health**

The 1960s and the early 1970s were years of change for the Massachusetts Department of Mental Health (DMH). The primary task of the department had historically been the maintenance of the mentally ill in institutions. Beginning in the early 1960s, the idea that this should be the major role of the department began to be subjected to scrutiny both by those inside the department and by critics within the state administration and in mental health interest groups. Public opinion about to what extent and how government should be responsible for mental health became divided. As a result, like that of the Department of Public Works, the definition of the mission of DMH underwent major changes during this period. However, unlike the change in the Department of Public Works, which the governor used as a vehicle to establish his control over the department, the change in DMH involved little gubernatorial intervention. Instead, DMH during this period of change was a department on which Sargent had little personal impact. The issue of managing DMH seldom reached his agenda; and when it did, he was unable to make the department perform as he would have liked. Unlike the Department of Public Works, where he associated himself closely with the policy outcomes of the department, Sargent conciously avoided close contact with DMH, having recognized early in his term that the department held little promise for immediate or significant response to his direction.

Before examining the nature of Sargent's relationship with the Department of Mental Health, it is necessary to understand both the general organizational traits of DMH and the kind of management problems it posed for Sargent. These are examined in the first two sections of the chapter. The final section deals with Sargent's involvement with the department. It also looks at some of the reasons that chief executives may be unable and/or uninterested in managing agencies like DMH, for which they are nominally responsible.

DMH: Background and Description

Unlike many other state agencies for which central administrative structures were created and then followed by local branches or extensions, the Massachusetts Department of Mental Health was created in 1938 to control a series of locally based hospitals and facilities that were already in place. The first mental health facility in Massachusetts was the Worcester State Hospital, established in 1833. The construction and maintenance of the hospital were financed by the state with local aid for individual patients. State assumption of responsibility for the mentally ill was considered a major social reform. Throughout the early nineteenth century, a group of reformers led by Horace Mann and Dorothea Dix had urged that the mentally ill, who were frequently lodged in jails or county poorhouses, be provided with places to live where they could lead their lives with dignity and order.[1] They eventually persuaded legislators that the state should accept responsibility for the mentally ill, as it had done for other victims of long-term illnesses. The establishment of the Worcester Hospital was followed by the construction of nine other state hospitals in the nineteenth and early twentieth centuries, the last of which was Gardner State Hospital in 1902.

The hospitals were overseen by a State Board of Charities, a part-time board created in 1864. This board was replaced by the State Board of Lunacy and Charities in 1879, which in turn was replaced by the State Board of Insanity in 1898. It was not until 1904 that these statewide bodies had any real power over the management of the institutions, however. For the first seventy years of their existence, the hospitals were autonomous institutions managed by individual hospital superintendents.

During the late nineteenth century the nature of the institutions began to change. As waves of immigrants moved into cities and rapid social changes mixed heterogeneous groups of people together in crowded circumstances, the number of people declared "insane" began to swell; and the state hospitals became overcrowded and understaffed. In the early nineteenth century the Massachusetts state hospitals had been able to show a "recovery rate" of about 50 percent,[2] but by the early twentieth century the hospitals were publicly acknowledged to be little more than custodial institutions. Once considered the vanguard of social reform, the hospitals during the early twentieth century began to be perceived as "snake pits" and "warehouses" that primarily served the function of keeping the mentally ill segregated from the rest of the population.

By the early 1950s, the nature of the care of the mentally ill in large hospitals had become once again a major issue of social concern across the country. In 1955, Congress created the Joint Commission on Mental Illness and Health to study and make recommendations for changes in the mental health service delivery system. Chaired by the Massachusetts Commissioner of Mental Health, the commission recommended that patients be moved out of large hospitals and into networks of mental health programs in communities.[3] The idea of moving patients from hospitals into community mental health centers was given a further boost by President Kennedy, who proposed legislation that Congress passed as the Community Mental Health Centers Act of 1963. Massachusetts used funds made available by this legislation to study how community mental health centers could be set up. In 1966, the Massachusetts legislature passed the Comprehensive Mental Health and Retardation Services Act (Chapter 735), which divided the state into seven regions and thirty-nine areas, designated to be the base of a new mental health system designed to bring patients out of the large state hospitals and back to smaller, "more humane" community facilities.

The structure of the department established in Chapter 735 is a complicated one with many layers of personnel. The chief executive officer of the department is the commissioner, who is appointed by the governor. Though in 1973 the legislation dictating the job specifications for the commissioner was changed to allow nonphysicians to hold the postion, traditionally the commissioner has been a psychiatrist. The department's second-in-command is the deputy commissioner, who by law must be a psychiatrist. In addition, the commissioner's office consists of assistant commissioners for community programs, mental retardation, research, administrative services, drug rehabilitation, and children's services.

Even including the staffs of the assistant commissioners, the staff of the central office of the department numbers about three-hundred and fifty, a fraction of the total of eighteen-thousand people the department employs. Each of the department's seven regions has its own administrator, who theoretically controls all facilities and programs within his region and who is responsible to the central office. The seven regions are in turn divided into thirty-nine areas, each of which has a director and a twenty-one-member citizen advisory board. Though the area structures have existed since 1967, they have always operated with very limited funding and often hospital superintendents and clinic directors have served concurrently as directors of mental health area programs.

The department is not only dispersed geographically but also fragmented because it provides a large number of different kinds of services and programs. The department's eleven state hospitals for the mentally ill and five state schools for the retarded each has a superintendent who is responsible for the administration of the institution. In addition, the department runs or funds mental health centers, mental health clinics, alcoholism treatment centers, drug rehabilitation programs, geriatric programs, court clinics, day care centers, clinical nursery schools, and a variety of community residences for those coming out of institutions.

Most of the department's budget, $193 million in the 1975 fiscal year, still goes to running the department's large mental hospitals and the state schools for the retarded. Approximately 75 percent of the total appropriation for the 1974 and 1975 fiscal years was spent on the hospitals, and of this approximately 90 percent was used to pay salaries.[4] The fixed costs of running the hospitals is extremely high, with only about 10 percent of the total cost of the department's budget for institutions subject to any kind of management or policy changes.

What this means in practical terms is that there is very little room for discretion over how the largest part of the budget is spent as long as the department continues to operate the large institutions. Although the population of the mental health hospitals decreased from 18,433 in 1962 to approximately 7000 in 1973,[5] maintenance costs of the institutions and inflation have caused the costs of running the institutions to remain constant.

Since 1904, when the commonwealth assumed full responsibility for the mentally ill,[6] the state has provided the bulk of government funding for public care of the mentally ill. Localities often pay for a small share of mental health clinics and health centers and provide funds for drug treatment and alcoholism facilities (to which DMH also contributes), but their share of the total cost of the department's programs is minimal. The federal government traditionally has stayed out of the field of provision of mental health services by the state and has directed most of its grants-in-aid to research or training programs. The National Institutes of Health granted approximately $22 million in research and staffing grants to Massachusetts in fiscal year 1975,[7] but most of these monies went to universities, hospitals, or clinics affiliated with the department and in no way covered the department's annual operating expenses. The state also received federal Hill-Burton funds for hospital construction and less than $10 million annually for development of community mental health centers. In addition, approximately 25 percent of the department's budget is federally reimbursable through the Medicaid, Medicare, and Supplemental Security Income provisions of the Social Security Act. All Social Security reimbursement is funneled through the Department of Public Welfare, however, and does not figure in the department's annual operating budget. Because most of the federal government's funding of the department is indirect, either through training and staffing grants or through Medicaid and Medicare, the relationship between the department and various federal agencies has not traditionally been a tight one. Unlike the Department of Public Welfare or the Department of Public

Works, the Department of Mental Health is funded primarily with state funds appropriated annually by the legislature.

Of the department's eighteen-thousand employees, fewer than 1 percent are not subject to protection by the state civil service system. Although professional employees do not always have to be hired from civil service lists for positions, once they are hired almost all employees enjoy civil service protection. In order to dismiss an employee, the commissioner must go through the complicated and often long grievance procedures laid down by the Civil Service Commission. In effect this means the commissioner has only a small number of central staff positions into which he can place his own appointees. This limitation on the commissioner's power to put his own employees in positions at all levels of the department has produced a system where administrators, especially superintendents, stewards, and business managers at the hospitals and state schools, have tended to stay for a long time. This protection from direction from the central administration has been increased because of the small size of the central office staff and has reinforced the autonomy of the administrators of the large institutions in making personnel and policy decisions.

The majority of high administrative posts in the department are held by psychiatrists. The posts of commissioner, deputy commissioner, assistant commissioners for medical programs, hospital superintendents, and regional directors have traditionally been held by psychiatrists.[8] The rationale for putting psychiatrists in these posts has always been that the department performs functions that are primarily medical and that it is therefore crucial to have technically competent physicians in decision-making positions. This fact accounts for a number of distinctive features of the department's structure and administration. First, medical training has always been considered at least as important a qualification for the top administrative jobs in the department as administrative or management experience. Second, although the top administrative jobs in the department are filled by medical personnel, the total number of doctors in the department is very low. The vast majority of department employees are involved in the maintenance and nonmedical operations of the department's institutions. The gap in training and experience between the majority of the department's personnel and the doctors in administrative positions is large. Even among the medical personnel the distinction between physician-administrators, who supervise the central office and the hospitals, and the doctors who fill staff positions in the hospitals is great. The position of staff psychiatrist in the state hospitals has always carried with it a low salary and an extremely high patient/doctor ratio. The result has been that more than 50 percent of the staff physicians in hospitals are graduates of foreign medical schools and many hold these jobs because they are unable to qualify for private practice.[9] Of the 375 positions available for doctors in the department in 1974, only 49 were filled by licensed physicians. The turnover in these positions is extremely high. Thus, the top of the hierarchy in the department consists of a small "administrative class" of psychiatrists who hold managerial positions in the central office or positions as hospital superintendents. They are responsible for the large institutions, the majority of whose personnel have jobs and training that in no way resembles their own.

The kind of services the department delivers and the fact that it delivers them throughout the state primarily through institutions dictates the nature of the department's constituencies. The legislature has always maintained a lively interest in the department. There are a number of easily identifiable reasons for this. First, the department's budget is large and its institutions are decentralized and highly visible to local constituencies. Second, the department's institutions and programs provide services of great importance to the citizens who need them and, if accessible to a legislator, can be a valuable source of constituent services and jobs. Although the janitorial or maintenance jobs in institutions to which a legislator might have access are not as much in demand as they once were, they are still a source of interest to legislators who need to find temporary employment for constituents. In addition, because the demand for places in state schools for the retarded and in various mental health facilities is far greater than the supply, legislators who are familiar with the administration of the department and of the facilities in their district can often help place constituents or their relatives in DMH institutions.

Finally, the legislature has stayed in touch with the department because there have always been some legislators in both the Senate and the House who have made mental health and mental retardation "their" issue. Many of the issues surrounding how the mentally ill and the retarded are cared for are highly salient and can generate public outcry and media attention. Charges that children are being excluded from treatment, that the condition of state facilities is poor, or that the mentally ill are being loosed on communities are issues of interest and concern to local constituencies. Several legislators always seem to have a genuine concern with the plight of the mentally ill and the retarded. This has meant that the department and its services have been featured prominently on the legislature's agenda and have been the focus of much legislation and of many special legislative commissions and investigations.

Because the department provides medical services and filters many training and research grants to hospitals and universities, the Massachusetts medical community has always been an active constituent of the department. The commissioner and the chief administrators of the department have traditionally been psychiatrists, so professional ties between the department and the medical schools and research institutions have been tight. Because an important job of the department is provision of medical and psychiatric services, the professionals in the state at prestigious private institutions for years have been involved in such tasks as evaluating the competence of the candidates for the job of commissioner and setting and monitoring the medical and professional standards of the department. In addition, Massachusetts organizations of physicians have always supported keeping the department a "medical" institution and insulating it as much as possible from the usual government pressure for economy, efficiency, and accountability to political bodies rather than to medical standards.

There has also always been a variety of well-established consumer and lay groups active in the government of mental health. Each mental health area in Massachusetts has a twenty-one-member area board that concerns itself primarily with local and community mental health services. Many board members are citizens who became involved with the issue of mental health in the 1950s when it had a renaissance as an important issue of social reform. There are also many relatives or friends of the mentally ill or mentally retarded on these boards. Although in theory these boards have a mandate to rank priorities for mental health services in their areas, it was not until the 1975 fiscal year that they had any technical staff or sympathetic support in the central office of DMH. As a result, they have generally had only a limited impact on the budgetary process.

There are several other organized lay groups generally interested in mental health, such as the Massachusetts Association for Mental Health, many of whose more than five hundred members are also involved in mental health area boards. In addition to these general purpose organizations, there are also many groups especially concerned with particular services provided by the department. The Massachusetts Association for Retarded Citizens (MARC), the Association for Mentally Ill Children (AMIC), and the Massachusetts Association for Learning Disabilities are among the largest and most powerful of these groups. There are also a whole series of mental health advocacy groups that began to flourish in the late 1960s. Many of these groups, such as the Massachusetts Committee on Children and Youth, the Task Force on Children Out of School, and the Massachusetts Advocacy Center, have focused their attention on children and have staffs and a research capability. Their strongest weapons have been the salience of their cause for the media and their ability to bring law suits and find redress for their grievances in the courts. Several of the more established large special interest groups such as MARC have adopted many of the new advocacy groups' tactics and as a result have made their causes increasingly public and political.

The Management of the Department

The 1960s marked a period of change in the climate of opinion about what the nature of government's obligations to and treatment of the mentally ill should be. Though it is impossible to pinpoint what caused attitudes to change about who should be involved in decision making about mental health and about what kinds of treatment were most humane and most effective, it is clear that this change did occur. Both the Congress and the president began to provide some national leadership for the community mental health movement and gave some focus to the general dissatisfaction with the overcrowded and often inhumane conditions in large mental hospitals and institutions for the retarded. Professionals and constituent groups who had been concerned with mental health for years began to question the assumption that large hospitals were the best medical or social solution to the problem of treating the mentally ill. In addition, as they had in other areas of government social programming, citizen groups began to demand that they play a larger role in the decision making on issues of mental health policy that involved their communities.

Like the Department of Public Works, the Department of Mental Health was being asked during this period to respond to demands that it change its way of operating and the definition of its primary task, running large institutions. The nature of the changes demanded of DMH were different in one especially significant way from demands for change in the Department of Public Works, however. Pressure for change in the Department of Public Works coalesced around one major issue: whether to build a set of highways. For the Department of Mental Health, the issues at stake were more complicated. The prevailing opinion seemed to be that large hospitals were ineffective and inhumane, but alternative solutions to the problem of what could be done with the mentally ill and the retarded were unclear. Both citizen groups and professionals knew what they did not want—large hospitals that served as "warehouses" and were immune to community and citizen involvement and control—but what specific kinds of programs and administrative structures could replace these was less clear. The issue involved formulating a program to dismantle a huge administrative apparatus directed primarily at running large institutions and replacing it with one that could still serve equal numbers of people, provide "quality" care in individual communities, and ensure local participation in decision making about how that care should be provided. On the DMH agenda were no clear programs or goals but, instead, a series of disparate and often conflicting suggestions about what an ideal mental health system might do.

When Sargent became acting governor in 1969, the commissioner of mental health was Milton Greenblatt, who had been appointed in 1967 by Sargent's predecessor, John Volpe. The term of office for a commissioner was four years, and until 1972 the commissioner's appointment was not coterminous with the governor's term. The job of commissioner of mental health had been considered primarily a professional position rather than a political one; and during the 1950s and 1960s, Massachusetts governors, regardless of their party, had normally reappointed the incumbent commissioner unless he expressed some desire to leave. Greenblatt's predecessor, Dr. Harry Solomon, had served in the position since 1958, and when he announced his intention to resign, a committee of professionals and citizens was set up to assist the governor in the search for a new commissioner. The committee recommended Greenblatt to Volpe, who appointed him in 1967.

The job of commissioner in Massachusetts was regarded as one of the most prestigious administrative posts in the field of health in the country, and Greenblatt's credentials satisfied demands both for professional achievement and administrative experience. A graduate of Harvard Medical School, Greenblatt had done extensive scholarly research while he was assistant director of the Massachusetts Mental Health Center, one of the leading psychiatric research centers in the country. He had also taught at Harvard Medical School. At the time he was offered the job of commissioner, he was superintendent of Boston State Hospital, the largest of the state's hospitals, with a staff of more than one thousand.

The appointment was widely hailed as a good one. Given the nature of the job of commissioner at that time and the nature of the qualifications traditionally required, the choice of Greenblatt seemed perfect. At the same time as the Greenblatt appointment, however, some of the changes in the climate of opinion about mental health and about how government should handle it were beginning to have repercussions in the department. In 1967, the department had begun to set up the citizen area boards mandated by the 1966 legislation reorganizing the department. Though it was unclear exactly what the power of these area boards was to be, it was clear that they were intended to break down the autonomy in decision making enjoyed by hospital superintendents and administrators in the central office and to balance off professional expertise with citizen involvement. The task of striking this balance and of fitting the newly organized and vocal boards into an old and insulated organizational structure fell to Greenblatt.

At the same time proposals for another significant change in the organization of the department were also beginning to be generated. In 1969, the General Court passed a sweeping reorganization package requiring that all agencies report to cabinet-level secretariats. Despite the opposition of the department, DMH was designated to be included in the new Executive Office of Human Services. The legislation mandated that in 1970 human services was to become the umbrella agency for mental health and that the commissioner was to report through the secretary of human services to the governor. Thus, in effect, two new levels of government had been added to the already complex mental health structure—citizen boards at the bottom and a superagency between the commissioner and the governor.

Sargent was elected to a full four-year term as governor in 1970, and in the early summer of 1971 he appointed Peter Goldmark to be the first secretary of human services. Goldmark was a former assistant director of the New York City Budget Bureau and a former assistant to John Lindsay. His primary experience was with budgetary and fiscal problems and with management and analysis of a variety of programs. He was young, from out of state, and not a doctor; and it was to him and his new staff that Greenblatt, who was accustomed to being accountable to his professional colleagues and, when necessary, to the governor, was to report.

It soon became clear that the nature of the job of commissioner had changed considerably since Greenblatt had taken it in 1967. Although Goldmark recommended Greenblatt's reappointment to another term when Greenblatt's first term expired only three months after Goldmark took office, the pressures for change in the department both from Goldmark and from various constituency groups placed a whole new set of demands on Greenblatt. One of Goldmark's objectives, shared by Sargent, was to move as many people as possible out of the large human services institutions such as mental hospitals, prisons, and juvenile correctional facilities and into smaller community-based facilities and programs. Though he agreed in principle with these objectives, Greenblatt had served as the superintendent of a large hospital and was reluctant to move hastily to close hospitals or to fire or transfer staff, especially when the alternatives to hospitalization were not yet clear or proved. In addition, Greenblatt had spent years in a mental health system dominated by professional organizations and by nonmilitant special interest groups such as the Massachusetts Association for Mental Health. He was therefore much less prepared to listen sympathetically than Goldmark was to the new strident advocacy groups that were beginning to emerge. In 1972, one of these groups, the Task Force on Children Out of School, published a report called *Suffer the Children* that severely criticized the department's services for and treatment of children.[10] Greenblatt's response to the report was first to urge the foundation that had supported the report to suppress it. When that failed, he publicly dismissed the conclusions as unfounded and based on poor research and said that he would ignore it. He refused to respond to the report until Goldmark drafted a public statement for Greenblatt to make.

At the same time, additional new demands were being made on the department by the courts. An Amherst activist named Benjamin Ricci had filed suit against the department in 1972, alleging that conditions and staff at the Belchertown State School for the Retarded were inadequate. Courts all around the country were beginning to follow the example laid down in the Federal District Court's decision in *Wyatt* v. *Stickney*[11] and to order states to remedy inadequate conditions in state-controlled institutions. In *Ricci* v. *Greenblatt*, the court issued a consent decree saying that the department had to bring Belchertown up to a higher standard of care by hiring more staff and by updating its facilities.[12] Following Ricci's example, a variety of constituent and advocacy groups began to make demands on Greenblatt and the department to improve the quality of the large institutions and to use as their weapon the threat of suits. These demands were usually directed at improving particular facilities rather than at improving all mental health services equally. Greenblatt, who was operating with a budget already stretched to try to cover provision of the customary mental health services, was unable and unwilling to respond to these demands except in instances where he was specifically directed to do so by the courts.

The locally based mental health area boards were also beginning to be highly critical of Greenblatt. Because the mental health system was decentralized and because the intent of Chapter 735 had been to create citizen boards to reflect local interests, these boards had become advocates for particular mental health and retardation programs and facilities in their own areas. Because their demands had to be filtered through so many levels of the mental health bureaucracy and because their access to the central office and to the expertise necessary to understand how decisions were made there was limited, many of the boards felt the department and Greenblatt were inaccessible. Greenblatt's ability to control the institutions on which most of the area board concerns were centered was limited both by their autonomy from the central office and by state civil service and personnel procedures. In addition, as the chief operating officer of the entire mental health system, he had a difficult time satisfying area board demands, which by their very nature were specific, localized, and not formulated with statewide objectives in mind.

A final incident capped the rising tide of pressure on Greenblatt from citizen groups and from the secretariat. Within four weeks in November and December of 1972, four residents at the Belchertown State School died. The department conducted its own investigation of the deaths and found that they were unavoidable and were in no way the result of departmental negligence. The press and a group of parents of Belchertown residents questioned the department's findings insistently enough that the governor appointed a special commission headed by Goldmark to investigate the matter further and to find out specifically who could be held responsible for the deaths. Eventually the commission placed part of the responsibility for the deaths on Greenblatt. Though by the time the commission made its findings public he had resigned from his job, simply the fact that his own department's report and his own responsibility in the matter were being called into question added further pressure to the job of commissioner.

In December of 1972, Goldmark and Sargent agreed that they should try to persuade Greenblatt to resign.[13] Buffeted by a department that was changing rapidly but in no single clear direction, by new constituency groups with which he had few natural ties, and by a superior who wanted to move the department more quickly and in different directions than he did, Greenblatt left his post.

The search for a new commissioner was a prolonged and difficult one. Legislation had been passed to make the appointment of the commissioner coterminous with the election of the governor, so the new commissioner would be stepping into an appointment guaranteed for only the year left in Sargent's term. In addition, there was legislation pending before the General Court that, if passed, would take away the regulatory functions of the department, remove services for the mentally retarded to a new department, and combine the administration of the mental hospitals with that of the public health hospitals. There was also a general atmosphere of uncertainty about what the department was supposed to *do* and therefore what kind of commissioner the search committee should be looking for. Various groups were pressuring the department to close down the hospitals, to provide more services, to plan carefully for community residences, to manage more efficiently and more tightly, to ensure greater citizen participation, and to serve a variety of other goals, many of which were often directly contradictory to the goals of other groups. Pressure was also building to have a commissioner whose primary experience and training had been administrative and political rather than medical; and in the spring of 1973, as the search was being conducted, the General Court abolished the requirement that the commissioner be a board-certified psychiatrist.

After a six-month search conducted by a panel of citizens and medical professionals, Sargent appointed William Goldman, a San Francisco psychiatrist, to the job. Goldman had gone to medical school in Boston but had spent most of his professional career in California, where he had been director of a community mental health center and a leader of the national movement to establish a network of community mental health centers around the country. He had none of the scholarly credentials usually characteristic of the commissioner in Massachusetts. He had made his reputation as an advocate of community participation and representation in decision making on health-related matters. Though by the end of the Sargent administration he had just become fully acquainted with the Massachusetts mental health system, he was neither reticent to speak out on the need for change nor reluctant to make clear where he stood. During the first six months that he was in his job he made two major decisions that set a tone for the department under his administration. The first was actively to involve the citizen area boards in the budget-making process by honoring the priorities they established in making up the department budget. The second tone-setting decision was to refuse to curry favor with the scholarly psychiatric community and, indeed, often to identify them as roadblocks to change. He especially agitated them by refusing to fund psychiatric residencies at many of the prestigious university hospitals and clinics and by diverting the funds for these residencies to the state hospitals.

By the end of the Sargent term, although he had been in office little more than a year, Goldman had already established himself as an often controversial personality who knew what he wanted and was perfectly willing to shake things up to get it. According to Goldman, this choice of style was a calculated one, geared to the nature of the department and its management problems.

What this department needs is unambiguous authority. Nobody knew what the hell they were supposed to be doing. I can't promise that I have the right answers, but at least I could give some leadership to people who didn't know where to turn.

I wanted to establish that the citizens were going to have some control over the department and that there was nothing sacrosanct about the medical community. I don't go in for the consensus mentality which has dominated this department for years. It's fine if you don't intend to do anything, but by pursuing a consensus you lose years. It's better to let everybody know where you stand and to shove yourself and the department out onto the firing line. Everybody here is desperate to have somebody to follow. That's the only way to manage this department—by leading it.[14]

The Goldman strategy was geared to making decisions in an environment filled with uncertainty. Perhaps the most significant thing about the Department of Mental Health during the Sargent administration was that what the department was supposed to do was ambiguous and that ambiguity was the result of a variety of problems that made management of the department extremely difficult. Like the Department of Public Welfare, the Department of Mental Health has a broad social objective, that of making the population of the state "mentally healthy." This objective can never be fully achieved or adequately measured and defined. Instead of relying on this as an objective, the department has always been forced to refine this into a series of more immediate short-term objectives that can change dramatically over time. In the nineteenth century, social reformers worked for fifty years to open hospitals for the mentally ill. By the beginning of the 1960s, the department's major objective had been reversed. The rhetoric of reform was directed at the need to "deinstitutionalize" the mentally ill. In addition to causing radical changes in the overall definition of the task of the department, this change also posed a set of real operational questions, such as how a large organization could deliver services to population bases instead of through large institutions and how hospitals and state schools could be maintained for those who always need institutional care.

The difficulty of managing the department and the ambiguity of goals during the Sargent administration was compounded by the fact that the program of moving patients from institutions into smaller community settings was experimental in nature. Because it was not an activity that had been tried on a large scale before, no one knew what the results of it would be or what was the best way to carry it out. The fact that government might be held responsible for causing a change with uncertain consequences placed the department in a particularly vulnerable position. The vulnerability of the department to community and electoral reaction against a government-sponsored social experiment reinforced the natural tendency of personnel of large organizations under fire to maximize their own security by doing nothing.

Unlike the change in mission in the DPW, the change in DMH did not make the department more amenable to management.

The department had not historically been a "task-oriented" bureaucracy because quality or quantity of service or criteria for performance were difficult to measure. Instead, the department had been "role-oriented," that is, expectations of how jobs should be performed were generated more by the history and structure of the department than by number or quality of discrete tasks performed. For example, superintendents in the department, unlike engineers in the DPW who measure their success by completion of a particular project like a road, had no fixed number of patients to cure or programs to see through to "completion." Instead they took their cues on successful performance of their jobs from the performance of their predecessors. This made change especially difficult.

The job of managing the department during the Sargent administration was further complicated by the importance of professionalism. There is a natural tension built into any strongly professional agency that operates under government control between providing services that meet the professional definition of excellence ("good mental health care," in the case of DMH) and providing services that are judged by the criteria often applied to the performance of government, such as accountability, efficiency, or economy. In the case of DMH this tension was particularly strong because the chief administrators of the department, who were psychiatrists, reported to a secretary and a governor whose professional experience had been in management, not medicine. As one senior administrator in the department put it:

To us, it often seems as if these "managers" are simply another level of government which exists to say "no" to what we think is good for patients and to push us to do things that are medically not sound. I firmly believe that it's easier to teach a psychiatrist management than to teach a manager psychiatry and that the department should be managed by being held accountable by generalists only if we do something grossly wrong.[15]

This sense of the propriety of allowing medical experts considerable autonomy over how the mental health system should run was reinforced by the nature of the decentralized hospital structure. The hospitals were in place long before any central authority was exercised over them, and in such a setting the superintendents came to be regarded in the institutions as both the chief medical officers and the chief administrators. This tendency to look to administrator-physicians for leadership was intensified because DMH had never had a group of middle-level managers with administrative skills or experience in either the hospitals or the central department, so that both the major administrative decisions and the major professional decisions had always been made by psychiatrists.

The job of running the department in the Sargent administration was also complicated by the fact that while the mission of the department was changing, the nature of its constituents, both supporters and opponents, was also changing. Citizen advocacy groups, because they wanted specific goods for particular groups, tended to make absolute demands on the department. During the early 1970s, they made these demands in the form of suits, using the courts as a threatened or actual means of forcing the department to provide redress for their grievances. At the same time, the citizen groups who had been more moderate in their demands and who had supported the orderly achievement of change were at a loss to define exactly what overall goals they wanted the department to serve. The mental health area boards were both frustrated about their lack of influence over the department and most concerned with local issues with little salience for their counterparts around the state. This fact made it difficult to organize them around any single set of goals.

In addition, although horror stories about conditions in mental hospitals had potential for generating a general public outcry, these incidents during the Sargent administration were confined to particular hospitals and were more often short-lived local controversies than statewide scandals that provoked a widespread sense of crisis. It was also difficult to organize vocal constituencies around general mental health goals because agreeing on and articulating what mental health policy should be was more difficult than it had been twenty years before. This policy no longer involved only questions of whether conditions or treatment for individuals who were locked away in hospitals or state schools should be changed. Instead, citizens were asked to agree on whether and how local communities and neighborhoods could accommodate the retarded and the mentally ill.

The Governor and DMH

From 1965 until 1975, the tasks of the Department of Mental Health were changing, disparate, and almost impossible to define, and this was why Francis Sargent did not manage the department. But Sargent's lack of involvement with DMH was also partly the result of Sargent's own choice not to become involved, a choice conditioned by his own style and interests and by the fact that he could have gained little and lost much by actually intervening. These factors, combined with the scarcity of crisis issues of statewide significance involving DMH during his term, meant that he was able to leave the department alone.

Early in his administration, Sargent explicitly delegated the management of the department and of mental health and retardation services to Goldmark. Mental health was not covered consistently as an issue by anyone on the governor's policy staff. This was not true, as it was in the case of the DPW, because Sargent had a trusted source of expertise elsewhere. No one in the Sargent administration was an acknowledged "expert" on mental health. Except for giving constant and explicit support for his policy of "deinstitutionalization," which involved many agencies in addition to DMH, Sargent's stands and statements on mental health were essentially reactive. His dealings with the Department of Mental Health were generally the result of situations in which he had to take some action or make some response, either to handle a potential political crisis brought to him by the public (as in the case of Russell Daniels or the deaths at the Belchertown State School) or to make a decision generated by the regular functioning of the bureaucracy (such as the selection of the new commissioner). In both of these kinds of situations, he resisted involvement for as long as possible, attempting instead to delegate responsibility.

The case of Russell Daniels was an example of a turbulent situation that eventually threatened to become a major issue in the election and therefore came to be treated by the governor as a crisis issue. Russell Daniels, a twenty-eight-year-old former resident of the Belchertown State School, had been released to a half way house in 1970. In 1973 he was accused of the murder of an eighty-three-year-old woman. He signed a confession, was convicted of second degree murder, and was sent to Norfolk Prison. In February of 1973, Benjamin Ricci, the president of the Friends of the Belchertown State School and a well-known and vocal advocate for the retarded, wrote a letter to Sargent arguing that Daniels's confession had been coerced and signed without counsel. In the same letter he requested that Sargent appoint a citizen commission to study the case and also to study the department's programs and policies to prepare residents for living in communities.

Sargent's office referred the letter to Goldmark's office for "appropriate action." The letter was misplaced in Goldmark's office and no response was made until a follow-up letter from Ricci was received in October. Goldmark's staff informed Ricci that the matter had been referred to the regional mental retardation administrator and that legal and personal counseling had been, and would continue to be, provided to Daniels.

In the meantime, the matter had begun to generate considerable public attention.[16] A WTIC documentary called "The Nine Year Old in Norfolk Prison" was aired in December and was followed by editorials in several papers and by angry letters to the governor and to Goldmark. Although Goldmark's office and DMH both had provided Daniels with counseling and were working diligently to have him retried (and, in the meantime, moved to a more appropriate program at Norfolk Prison), in April of 1974 a delegation of citizens and students from Amherst marched on the State House. They called on the governor to set up a commission to review police practices in Springfield, where Daniels had been arrested, and to investigate the Department of Mental Health's ability to carry out its responsibilities to retarded citizens. Sargent refused to meet with them at that time, though he agreed to meet with them in Amherst late in April.

Until the time of the meeting, the governor and his staff had not been involved in the case. Goldmark's staff had been working with DMH officials and had found that the department had done extensive follow-up on Daniels. They had had limited contact with anyone in the governor's office. The Daniels case had meanwhile become a "cause celebre" on the Amherst campus of the University of Massachusetts. Although staff members from Human Services and from DMH had documented the help Daniels had received, the Amherst group labeled them incompetent for having waited so long to respond to their initial letter and for being unable to move Daniels from Norfolk Prison. The issue appeared to be turning into a major controversy.

The day before the governor was to go to Amherst, after consulting with Goldmark and with his own staff, Sargent pardoned Daniels and released him to the Belchertown State School. Although a memorandum detailing the department's involvement with the Daniels case had been prepared for him for the meeting, Sargent made no attempt at the Amherst meeting to defend the department's record in the case and instead said that it was a situation beyond anyone's control.

The response to this statement was immediate. The following day, gubernatorial candidate Michael Dukakis met with the Friends of the Belchertown State School and called Sargent's statement "outrageous," State Senator John Olver made a public statement saying that "what pains me most is to see a governor come in here and say 'gee what can we do?' "[17] Sargent had not been intimately involved in the department's handling of the case and was not familiar with the details. Instead of defending his administration's handling of the case, which, with the exception of Human Services's failure to answer Ricci's initial letter, had been thorough, Sargent's response was to admit that "the Russell Daniels case was obviously poorly handled, what can I say?"[18] and to have his staff draft a fourteen-page response that essentially acknowledged the appropriateness of the citizen groups' demands.

Sargent did not have to take the blame on all crisis issues involving the department to which he had to respond. After the deaths of four residents of the Belchertown State School in 1972, the Department of Mental Health appointed a committee chaired by Deputy Commissioner Wilfred Bloomberg to investigate. This committee's finding that no one in the department was at fault so outraged several citizen groups and the press that the governor had to announce his intention to investigate the incidents. Rather than appointing an investigatory body composed of members not affiliated with the government, Sargent directed two of his own appointees, Goldmark and Secretary of Public Safety Richard McLaughlin, to conduct the investigation. Although he appointed the committee from among those inside the government and therefore attempted to retain some control over the investigatory process, Sargent and his staff made no effort to keep track of the progress of the investigation. The governor's office was not informed what the conclusions of that report were until the day before the commission finished its three-month investigation and presented its findings publicly. This was true although the commission concluded there had been negligence on the part of several state employees and recommended disciplinary action be taken against several of them including Commissioner Greenblatt, who was found to have been remiss because he had not designated an acting superintendent at Belchertown. By the time the commission announced its findings, Greenblatt had resigned; but the fact that an investigatory commission appointed by a governor had recommended action against one of his own commissioners was a widely reported subject of much public discussion. By remaining detached from the commission's proceedings, Sargent had kept some distance both from the bitterness in the department about the commission's findings and from being personally associated with the Belchertown deaths.

Sargent's reactive style and handling of mental health issues by "delegating" responsibility for them was characteristic not only on issues that posed an immediate political threat but also on other DMH management issues that reached him. The possibility of pushing Greenblatt out of the commissionership was surfaced first by Goldmark, and Sargent delegated the logistics of how to do it to him. Similarly, the search for a new commissioner was handled completely by Goldmark's staff and by the search committee of outside advisors that Goldmark appointed to help him. Although the choice of Goldman was ultimately Sargent's, he and one other candidate were the only two contenders whom Sargent or his immediate staff met.

The fact that Sargent himself took no initiatives in making policy for the Department of Mental Health is not necessarily a measure of his ineptitude or lack of concern about mental health. Although at times if he had known more about the workings of the department he could have taken credit for initiatives or, as in the Russell Daniels case, spared himself some criticism, removing himself from the department also had its benefits for him. It allowed him to keep his options open in deciding extremely difficult questions for far longer than he could have if he had been personally associated with the initiative. In addition, it allowed him to remain at arms length from a department that had always been regarded as difficult to manage and that was especially so as it underwent a basic change in its operations.

Perhaps the most compelling reason of all for Sargent to have remained uninvolved with the management of the department was that trying to manage a department like DMH offers few political or electoral rewards for a political executive. Because of the diffuse and complicated nature of its tasks, the Department of Mental Health, like the Department of Public Welfare, provides few opportunities for a governor to declare a program or an issue a success. The kinds of changes that would have allowed Sargent to control the department and to make it accountable to him would have involved slow, often technically complex procedural or personnel changes, such as the development of a strong group of middle-level managers in the institutions or reform of personnel and civil service regulations. These kinds of changes would have required large amounts of Sargent's time and his use of a good many political resources. As a chief executive elected for only four years and with limited resources, it would have been difficult to decide that he could afford such an attempt at control.

In Sargent's case, these electoral constraints were reinforced by his own personal style, which was not to involve himself in the often highly complex matters of internal reform of the administrative structure. He was not fond of managing bureaucratic detail. In addition, many of the most pressing issues in mental health also involved other departments, such as welfare or corrections, or other secretariats, such as the Executive Office of Elder Affairs, and would have involved his arbitration among agencies, a role he, like many other chief executives, disliked. Finally, the fact that the primary issue before the department in the Sargent administration was the transfer of people who had been in institutions into communities where they were feared meant that the potential for failure was great and could have immediate political repercussions for him.

The difficulty of the job of managing DMH and the nature of Sargent's own personal style help explain why his involvement with the department was limited. More important in explaining this is the fact that "crisis issues" involving the department were infrequent during Sargent's administration. Although there were many citizens interested in mental health, they did not agree on what the department's goals should be. In the absence of any general goals, and because of the highly decentralized and specific nature of constituent demands for change, there was no widely shared public sense of crisis. Unlike welfare, where public concern about the general purposes and management of the department was widespread and focused at the state level, mental health issues were handled by a decentralized department and characterized by localized grievances. Because of this absence of crisis, Sargent could afford to avoid risking political disaster by attempting to control the department and could instead ignore it except when specific incidents arose.

Notes

1

The historical material on the department is drawn primarily from Gerald Grob's excellent book, *The State and the Mentally Ill.* I have also relied on the *Report of the Massachusetts Mental Health Hospital Planning Project* and "Mental Health as a Government Service" by Charles Hamberg.

2

This figure comes from historical material on DMH supplied to me by William Gorsky, public relations officer for the Department of Mental Health.

3

Report of the Massachusetts Mental Hospital Planning Project, p. 10ff.

4

These figures were given to me by George Hertz, mental health budget analyst in the Executive Office of Human Services, and closely approximate those in the analysis section of *F.Y. '75 Budget: Summary of Programs and Recommendations of the Budget in English,* p. 88ff. Most of the information about the department's budget in the following paragraphs comes from these two sources.

5

These figures come from the files gathered by the Executive Office of Human Services for the proposal to reorganize the Department of Mental Health submitted to the legislature in the spring of 1973.

6

This was the result of the so-called "State Care Acts" (Mass., Acts of 1900, chap. 451; Acts of 1903, chap. 321).

7

Interview with Edward Sarsfield, special assistant to the commissioner of mental health for federal relations. All of the information about federal funding that follows comes from interviews with Sarsfield and Hertz.

8

Though by 1975 the statutory requirements that the commissioner and the hospital superintendents be physicians had been abolished, the majority of these posts were still filled by psychiatrists.

9

This information and the following information on foreign psychiatrists was supplied to me by Friendly Ford of the DMH Division of Research and Statistics. It is based on an investigation he had undertaken for the department.

10

Report of the Task Force on Children Out of School, *Suffer the Children.*

11

Wyatt v. *Stickney*, 325 F.Supp. 781 (M.D.Ala., 1971), 344 F.Supp. 373 (M.D.Ala., 1972).

12

Refer to the consent decree for *Ricci* v. *Greenblatt*, civil action no. 72-469-1 (US D.C.Mass., Nov. 12, 1973).

13

This whole scenario was based on an interview with Peter Goldmark and on my own observation of the situation. It is not clear whether Goldmark or the governor ever actually ordered Greenblatt to resign or whether the decision was actually Greenblatt's.

14

Interview with William Goldman, commissioner of mental health.

15

Interview with Deputy Commissioner Wilfred Bloomberg.

16

The account of the Russell Daniels incident is based on clippings from newspapers, memos in the files of the Executive Office of Human Services, and an interview with Jane Hughes, deputy assistant secretary for project management in EOHS.

17

Springfield *Republican*, April 21, 1974.

18

Francis Sargent quoted in the Amherst *Record*, April 24, 1974.

8
Conclusions

Like all governors, Francis Sargent aspired to a style of political leadership distinctive enough and effective enough to engage the attention and support of those whom he supervised, his fellow politicians, and the electorate. Though the tone and consistency of this leadership was to a certain extent a natural outgrowth of his personality and values, it also involved conscious calculation on his part. He made decisions about the allocation of resources and about his own personal priorities. Like all governors, he had to assess the extent and nature of his political and administrative power and decide how it could best be used. His brand of leadership was affected by decisions about political resources—whether they were transferable, timebound, or even real. Because of his position, his use of authority, and his skills, his preferences became important considerations in Massachusetts government. They were important because they had an impact on public policy and because they were one determinant of how Massachusetts government performed during Sargent's tenure in office.

But Sargent, like all governors, no matter how skilled or adroit, was not a master of his own destiny. How the executive branch of government performed during Sargent's tenure was not only a reflection of Sargent's leadership, behavior, and direction. The performance of the Sargent administration was also affected by many factors over which Sargent had no control. It was affected by the history and personality of the large organizations for which he was responsible and by the extent of congruence of Sargent's goals with their own. It was also affected by the political climate, the public's agenda, and issues "whose time had come." Therefore, in evaluating the Sargent years in Massachusetts politics it is necessary, in addition to looking at Sargent or at any single substantive policy area, to step back and look at why the many parts of the executive branch behaved as they did, how they affected each other, and what accounted for their policies.

The most important characteristic of elected chief executives, if the Massachusetts case is representative, is their reliance on crisis management. Chief executives may differ significantly from each other in style, in the kinds and amounts of resources available to them, and in the circumstances of their political environments. But all chief executives must maintain public or electoral support in order to be reelected or to extend and maintain their administrative authority. This means that their strategies for management of administrative agencies must be both sensitive enough to public concern (or to the executive's conception of that concern) to ensure that it is always given priority and flexible enough that they can be accommodated to the exigencies of unpredictable, often uncontrollable, agendas.

Though governors and their staffs in some instances may spend their time dealing with agencies on issues that have little potential for causing public or bureaucratic turmoil, these instances are the exception rather than the rule. Governors do not manage in the customary sense of the word, that is, they do not direct or oversee the affairs of agencies over some sustained period of time. Instead, management for elected chief executives usually involves sporadic intervention in the agencies' business, often only for a short period of time. This intervention is most often initiated because of a crisis.

Political crises cannot be defined by any objective standard. Though they are often signaled by sudden events of unpredictable and uncontrollable proportions, the most important distinguishing characteristic of political crises is that they are perceived to be critical events by a political executive or his staff. Any event that a governor thinks he must manage in order to retain or garner public support or to preserve an internally consistent, strongly felt set of values or goals may be a crisis. The model of crisis management, most simply put, maintains that the single variable most important in determining the style and content of a chief executive's dealings with his agencies is the presence or absence of crisis. Public perception of his success or failure at managing these crises may depend as heavily on his ability to "market" his handling of the situation as it does on the extent to which he has actually solved a problem.

The "crisis management" style of an elected chief executive does not involve equally steady oversight of all agencies. Instead, the executive focuses his attention on a limited number of agencies at one time. The crisis management style dictates that the most important feature of an agency for a governor is not necessarily its size or the policies with which it deals but, rather, the salience of the immediate issues with which it is dealing and the public's perception of those issues. The hallmark of a successful crisis manager is not the steadiness or thoroughness with which he deals with his agencies but, rather, his ability to intervene in the agency at the appropriate time, to muster resources quickly, and to convince the agency and the public that he has achieved some resolution of the problem. In effect, what this means is that gubernatorial intervention is limited and not evenhanded for all agencies. In agencies where there is no crisis, there often is no management on the part of the governor.

Recognizing the importance of crisis management for publicly elected chief executives is important in understanding why they make the kinds of decisions they do. Both the model of the rational decision maker who closely calculates the costs and benefits of his actions and the model of the decision maker who "muddles through" help explain the behavior of chief executives in certain situations.[1] But the crisis management model of decision making adds an additional dimension to the explanation of why a governor like Sargent behaves as he did. It also helps explain seeming inconsistencies in his behavior not predicted by either the rational actor model or the muddling-through model.

Elected chief executives do not often have the luxury of rationally calculating a long-range strategy for how to achieve their goals. Unlike the rational decision maker, they manage very few issues from their inception to their conclusion. The extent and timing of their intervention is dependent on their knowledge of the issue, on the resources available to them, and on what other things they must do at the time. Their agencies are by their very nature subject to public control, which means they cannot be controlled totally by the political executive. To the extent that a governor must be responsible to the public's concerns and preferences, he cannot insulate himself enough from those preferences to make a detailed and ordered calculation of his own priorities or allow himself to use all his resources to manage individual issues from their inception to their conclusion. Even if he had wanted to, Sargent could not have afforded to figure out a system of management innovation for the welfare system himself. The best he could do was intervene in the department's management at two times—when he ordered the switch to the flat grant and when he hired Minter as commissioner.

On the other hand, all governors make some calculation of values that transcend each particular situation. A primary value for them is maintenance of public support, which no governor knowingly sacrifices to the dictates of "incrementalism." In addition, the theory of muddling through does not take into account the fact that elected chief executives do not always make decisions that only marginally affect policies. The results of their decisions are often dramatic. In Massachusetts, for example, a highway network was stopped because of Sargent's decision. Sargent also supported the controversial decisions by subordinates to close the juvenile training schools and to deinstitutionalize the mentally ill. In addition, the incremental model postulates that policy making involves a process of successive approximations of some desired objectives. Though administrators with life tenure in their jobs may make policy this way, elected chief executives do not always have the luxury of getting a second or third chance at making policy, and they are often conscious of this when dealing with their agencies and the policies for which they are responsible.

The crisis manager is constrained by aspects of his environment that are not exclusive to either the rational decision-making model or the incremental model. All elected chief executives make decisions on the basis of limited information, which means that they are unable to evaluate all options open to them. The incremental theory takes this limitation fully into account. But chief executives are also constrained by scarcity of resources and they often calculate whether to hoard or to spend these resources or, if they are to be spent, where they should be directed. It is precisely this kind of closely calculated deliberate decision that the theory of muddling through would predict that governors do not or cannot make.[2]

Crisis management differs from these traditional theories of management and decision making in several other significant ways. One of the most important things neither of these theories can adequately predict is how the governor's agenda is set. The rational decision-making model assumes that administrators can control their agendas to the extent that they can handle a problem from beginning to end. But governors are not in control of their own agendas. Instead, there are many agenda setters in the public sector. Issues such as transportation policy or welfare policy may be raised by the public and may have to be dealt with even if they are issues over which a governor has no jurisdiction or authority. On the day after the 1974 gubernatorial election Francis Sargent asserted that he was defeated by "the price of hamburg," an issue about which the public was aroused but one he had few resources to manage.

The rational decision-making theory would lead one to assume that governors would have an especially good chance of calculating objectives and of managing those objectives on issues they place on their own agendas. This does not take into account that even if a governor places an issue on his agenda himself, he cannot always remove it at will. For example, in Massachusetts, Sargent was closely identified early in his full term with the deinstitutionalization of adult and juvenile offenders. When the prisons experienced serious rioting and several prisoners did not return from their furloughs in 1972 and 1973, it was difficult for Sargent to step back from the issue and allow anything but strong public feeling to dictate the speed with which he had to act. The rational policy-making theory of management assumes that an executive can calculate which issues he will deal with and at what tempo. The crisis management model, on the other hand, recognizes that elected public managers cannot set their own agendas but instead, at best, can intervene in the policy-making process at a time when they can have some influence over what decision is made.

A further problem with applying the rational policy-making model to the publicly elected chief executive is that it does not take into account the important ways in which the mechanism for setting his agenda is biased against innovation. Although the rational policy-making model would lead us to believe that most problems are equally factorable, it is clear from what we have learned about crisis management that some problems are easier to deal with than others. All governors are especially constrained in their ability to change the behavior of agencies. In all cases in which a governor attempts to change agency behavior, this attempt costs him something. He may achieve control, but at the cost of goodwill in the agency. For example, although Sargent was able to institute the flat grant in the Department of Public Welfare, he did it at the cost of having to overcome the resistance of agency personnel to a change in routine and at the cost of having to keep close watch over the agency's behavior. Winning a change in policy may also cost a governor in a more subtle way. He may be so pleased that the agency is behaving the way he wants it to behave that he continues to devote his attention and resources to it long after he has already achieved "control," in essence wasting his resources.

Attempts to manage innovation or change in the agencies may also be unsuccessful, and this, too, has its costs. Because the appearance of having control over an agency may often be as important as actually controlling it, once it becomes clear to the public or to agency personnel that the governor is unable to change the agency's behavior, he may in fact lose substantial influence over it or may drop in the public's esteem. Sargent faced this situation in dealing with the Department of Mental Health. Early in his term he advocated various programs of deinstitutionalization for both the mentally ill and the mentally retarded. When it became clear that he could not "solve" the management problems of the department, both the public and the agency personnel began to realize that he was not in control. The least costly strategy he was able to pursue in response was to attempt to disassociate himself from responsibility for the department.

The model of the decisionmaker who muddles through might predict that the elected chief executive would not be in control of his own agenda and that a decisionmaker at times can make only marginal adjustments in what policies are under consideration. It might also predict the strong bias against innovation in public sector agenda setting. However, this theory does not explain certain other equally important facts about elected executives. The crisis management model assumes the importance of public pressure to a governor and his need for electoral and bureaucratic support. This means that issues that call for dramatic changes in policy do at times get on a governor's agenda and that governors can make decisions that cause major changes. In addition, the muddling through model makes no provision for the fact that elected chief executives may make and enforce calculated decisions about which agencies and policies they will pay attention to or ignore. The most important variable on which this calculation is based is the potential for crisis. Political executives make explicit calculations about the allocation of their time based on this potential. They do not devote equal amounts of time or resources to every agency head who happens to walk through their door. This calculation may cause them to deal with agencies such as the Department of Public Welfare, which, were it not for its crisis potential, any governor might want to avoid. Governors may also calculate which agencies they will spend time on according to how these agencies satisfy their other criteria. They may deal with agencies that do not tax their resources or that bring them good news. For example, although Sargent did not expend resources to control MHFA, he followed the agency closely enough to know what it was accomplishing and that it was favorably regarded.

The theory of muddling through might predict that governors would not deal with certain agencies or policies, but it would not lead one to understand an equally important fact, that that avoidance is often calculated. Governors often consciously avoid dealing with policy decisions involving their agencies because the decisions are difficult, complicated, or, most important, have no electoral payoff. They may be successful or unsuccessful in this calculation, but that they make the calculation at all is important. They may avoid dealing with problems on which they might lose. For example, although it infringed increasingly on his management of transportation policy, Sargent did not go to war with the Massachusetts Port Authority because of its power and its political support. Governors may also avoid dealing with management questions that will not help them be reelected. For example, Sargent never worked hard at controlling the Department of Mental Health, not because he was unaware of any of the problems it posed but because of the complexity of the job, the lack of certainty of success, and the fact that he might not have anything tangible to show for his intervention at the end of his term of office.

The crisis management model implies delegation of managerial responsibility, but a kind of delegation that neither the rational nor the incremental model anticipates. Because all chief executives intervene only sporadically in agency affairs and in policy-making and do not involve themselves in day-to-day management except in the most extraordinary circumstances, actual agency supervision is delegated downward in the hierarchy. The rational policy-making model would take into account and encourage the possibility of explicit delegation of responsibility for specific disaggregated tasks. This model makes two assumptions that are not always valid in public sector management: that the designated manager has power and that he confers it on others. In fact, only a certain amount of any governor's authority can be delegated, even if he clearly wishes it to be. This was evident in the Sargent administration. The problem with having a staff that operated as a set of "ministers without portfolio" was that their right to make decisions had to be implicitly, and frequently explicitly, reaffirmed by the governor. Even in cases where the governor delegated responsibility to managers with line authority, it was clear to everyone involved that the governor sat on top of the hierarchy and that only he could put a final stamp of approval on a decision of his administration. The consequences of this for consistent and clear management of the agencies were often disastrous. Although Sargent delegated the authority to deal with all mental health issues to Goldmark, this delegation was not always evident or satisfactory either to the public or to the agencies. In the Russell Daniels case, for example, the citizens involved in the issue were able to deal around Goldmark with the governor, who apologized for staff work that he had not followed. The result was both demoralizing to the employees who had worked on the case and damaging to the governor.

The rational policy-making model would lead one to believe that to the extent problems are broken down and explicitly delegated they become more manageable. In fact, explicit delegation and disaggregation of public sector problems is not always possible or desirable. Because governors are ultimately held responsible for management of crisis situations, they must protect themselves in some situations by not delegating. Even in situations in which the designated manager is both skilled at what he does and totally loyal to the governor, delegation of authority may not guarantee an agency will run smoothly. For example, although Minter had both the skills and expertise the job of commissioner of public welfare required, the complicated nature of the department's task and the impossibility of defining what had to be done made the department impossible to "run." In addition, the nature of the problem may mean that although that problem could be delegated, the public will not allow such delegation to occur. Again, the issue of welfare, for which a large part of the public holds the governor personally responsible, is instructive.

The model of muddling through gives an equally distorted picture of delegation and its function in the public sector. Implicit in this model is the notion that power may be delegated by default and that this may limit an executive's control over potentially important decisions.[3] In fact, this is not necessarily the case. Delegation of all tasks except crises may be an extremely efficient way for an executive to use his scarce resources. Because he must ultimately value the support of the electorate, the "blinders" he imposes on himself by allowing responsibility to be parceled out without his explicit delegation of it may serve a useful function, that of ensuring that he becomes aware only of those issues about which the public cares most.

In addition, the muddling through model would assume that delegation of responsibility by an executive is done by default rather than by design. Although at times this may be the case, it ignores the situations in which an elected chief executive makes a conscious, calculated choice and is unable to affect the outcome of a situation not because of his own lack of effort but because of the nature of the job that has to be done. The things that limit a governor's ability to manage by delegating may be as much results of the constantly changing nature of the job of managing public sector agencies and the correspondingly varied array of talents that it requires as they are results of blindness or lack of calculation on the part of the executive. A governor may consciously delegate responsibility to a manager only to find that the task for which he is responsible has changed. Sargent selected Greenblatt to be commissioner of mental health, the task of the department changed, and Greenblatt was no longer the appropriate manager of the department. Even those who are superior managers when they are delegated authority in one situation may be disasters in others. Altshuler, White, and Minter were all strong managers in their particular fields, but they were by no means interchangeable. There is no evidence to indicate that Minter had the resources or skills necessary to run MHFA or that Altshuler could have managed the Department of Public Welfare with any success. One of the ultimate ironies the traditional decision-making models do not deal with but that is true of all governors is that they are expected by the public both to be able to discriminate among managers in terms of what highly particularistic skills they possess and, at the same time, as "general managers" of the government, are expected to supervise and control all agencies as if they possessed all of these talents themselves.

The single most important factor both the models of rational policy making and of muddling through fail to take into account is the importance of crisis in determining how a governor manages. Governors do not sit in their offices and explicitly lay out their goals, objectives, and plans in accordance with the rank order of their priorities. Nor do they muddle through their daily management duties by making incremental changes in policies in order to move gradually toward different goals. Instead they attempt to respond to the publicly generated or personally perceived stimulus of a crisis. The important question to ask about a political executive's management is, therefore, what dictates what a crisis is and, more particularly, how this affects a governor's dealings with his agencies.

The importance of crisis to publicly elected chief executives means that they do not have the luxury of concerning themselves only with the policy outcomes of agencies. The behavior of agency personnel may be as important to them as the policies of those agencies. For any given agency, the governor may have to be more concerned with the ability of agency personnel to please the public or with an agency's appearance of competence than with the actual policies for which it is responsible. This concern with an agency's behavior may vary in direct proportion to the number of "incidents" (as opposed to "issues") with which the agency has to deal. In Massachusetts, for example, one of the chief preoccupations of both the governor and of the personnel of the Department of Public Welfare has always been to make the agency appear to run competently and professionally and to anticipate the kinds of "incidents" that might lead the public to believe the department does not function smoothly.

Neither the rational policy-making model nor the muddling through model focuses on the distinction between "incidents" and "issues." Yet it is clear that the crisis management style of elected chief executives means that these executives must be as responsive to the incidents that generate concern among the public or important groups on a day-to-day basis as they must be to issues of long-term significance for policy. Although governors by definition have little control over the number or kind of incidents an agency may generate, these incidents and the agency's behavior may be as important as any policy issue with which that agency is dealing in determining the extent to which the governor satisfactorily manages the agency.

The crisis agenda of the elected chief executive must include time to deal with incidents as well as with issues. In recent years, that agenda has become increasingly varied and subject to change by any number of political forces. Until recently in the United States, the only administrative "crises" with which elected chief executives had to become involved were scandals or an agency's blatant inability to operate. Although it is impossible to pinpoint precisely when a change occurred in who could dictate what a crisis is for government, it is clear that during the 1960s and 1970s public groups were informed and concerned enough about certain administrative issues that they had to be taken seriously by any governor. Because the public or part of the public perceived crises on issues involving the Department of Public Works and the Department of Public Welfare, Sargent had to treat these issues as crises. In addition, during these years certain "technocratic" issues began to be seen as crises because of the proliferation of people with technical skills both inside the government and outside it who understood how the most complicated bureaucratic functions of the government were performed and who wanted these functions changed, adjusted, or protected. The increasing complexity of government machinery and the variety of jobs to be done meant that governors and other elected executives had to rely on technical experts, both in their own administrations and outside, to inform them when a problem had reached crisis proportions and tell them what should be done about it.

The importance of crisis management to any governor and the fact that what a crisis is may be defined by persons outside the governor's office conditions any governor's motivation for trying to control agencies. Governors do not try to manage all their agencies as if they were equally important. The usual argument of reformers for clear lines of responsibility and a well-defined span of control for public executives assumes that public executives need and want to focus on all parts of their administration. Governors do not do this, nor do they deal with whatever agency happens to come to their attention, as the incrementalists might predict. Instead, they intervene in those agencies where they perceive a crisis. Sargent felt compelled to deal with the DPW and the Department of Public Welfare; he left MHFA and the Department of Mental Health alone.

The need to manage crisis dictates to a large extent the agencies in which the governor intervenes. Whether he "succeeds" in managing these agencies depends on two other important factors, neither of which any governor can completely control. His success or failure depends on whether the public or specific interest groups perceive him to have managed successfully. This, in turn, is conditioned not so much by whether the governor has in fact attempted to intervene in the agencies as by the nature of the agencies themselves. Perhaps the most important weakness of many theories of decision making and management is that they assume organizations are the same and the skills necessary to manage them do not vary from agency to agency. This is not true in the public sector. Agencies are different from each other in their organizational style, in their history, and in their capacity to change.

There are at least two general features of all agencies that allow one to differentiate them from each other and that are important in determining how "controllable" they are. The first is the degree of clarity of their central task. It is clear from the case studies that the extent to which a governor or any manager is able to isolate what an agency does or what he thinks it is supposed to do affects both his ability to make decisions and the agency's and the public's perception of what the agency is supposed to do. The clearer and the more limited the goals of any agency, the more obvious the criteria for evaluating a manager's performance will be. One of the major differences between public and private bureaucracies is that in a public bureaucracy the ability to set goals and establish tasks is generally more widely shared than in the private sector. Even among public agencies, the number of persons and groups who set goals and identify tasks varies greatly from agency to agency. This variation accounts for many of the differences among agencies in the importance of constituencies to them and in the ability of a chief executive to get the agencies to behave as he would like.

A second important variable that differentiates one agency from another is the general climate in which individual organizations operate. Paul Lawrence and Jay Lorsch have argued that much of the variation among firms in the private sector can be explained by understanding differences in their "critical environments."[4] Critical environments are equally important for public sector organizations. The most important feature of the critical environment of all public agencies is their potential for being perceived as dealing with issues of crisis proportions. Public agencies can also be distinguished from each other in terms of the differing degrees of stability or instability in the demand for their product, in terms of levels of uncertainty, or in terms of support or opposition outside the agency.

Many of the differences in the degree of accountability to the governor of the four agencies studied can be explained by looking at these two variables. During the period in which Sargent was dealing with the DPW, it was clear that the most serious issue involving the department was whether the highways should be built. Sargent was able to control the department during this period because the task was clear and of crisis proportions and his action on that task involved stopping a program rather than initiating or implementing one. The fact that the department's mission was changing helped the governor and Alt-shuler get control of it. The burden of uncertainty in this case fell on the employees and worked in favor of gubernatorial control. Department personnel, for the first time in the years that they had been working there, did not know what they were supposed to do. This fact, combined with the respect for chain of command that had characterized the engineers in the department, meant that they were amenable to direction by a new commissioner who was an engineer.

At the same time, a new constituent group that opposed building more highways and was both sophisticated about the general operation of government and had access to considerable technical expertise was developing. The issue was not only clear but also had become the subject of heated public debate, forcing the governor to pay attention to the department. It was expedient for Sargent to make a decision; and with Altshuler's help he was able to do so in such a way as to change the agency's behavior and be perceived as having managed the crisis successfully.

Sargent had to deal with the Department of Public Welfare during his term of office because, like those of the DPW, the issues with which the department was dealing were crisis issues for the public. However, unlike the DPW, the Department of Public Welfare had no single, easily definable task or issue on which public concern was focused. The brunt of the burden of uncertainty about the department fell on those who were trying to manage it. They were not only uncertain what the measure of success in "promoting the public welfare" was, but they also could never be certain about whether their own measures of the effectiveness of the welfare department corresponded to the public's. The department was faced with a generally concerned public, but that public concern was not focused on any single resolvable issue. The goals of one segment of the public were often entirely different from those of other segments. For example, welfare recipients wanted higher benefits; other citizen groups wanted to cut welfare spending. Because there was a high level of public interest and feeling about the department, the handling of individual incidents had to take precedence over long-range policy issues. Support for any single policy initiative was diffuse, and anger over breakdowns in the system was widespread. Because of the difficulty of defining the job to be done and because of the perpetual atmosphere of crisis surrounding the department, the agency was especially susceptible to the need for crisis management and immune to most interventions on the part of the governor. Sargent could never satisfy the public that he had done a good job at "running" welfare. Because of the environment and because of the issue itself, the best he could do was to try to keep afloat from one crisis to the next. He was never able to convince the public that he had achieved any management "successes" in welfare, though he expended considerable energy on trying to persuade them that establishment of a vendor file and the installation of computers to expedite payments were significant changes in the department's management.

MHFA generated no crises during Sargent's term. Like the goal of the Department of Public Works at the time, the goal of MHFA was relatively simple to define. Its job was to lend money to developers who in turn built housing. MHFA's job was not only easy to define but was also less subject to public scrutiny and tinkering than DPW's, public welfare's, or mental health's. This was true for two reasons. First, its function as a public mortgage agency was highly complex and difficult for the general public to find out about or to understand. Most of those who understood how the agency worked were experts in housing, development, or banking; and most of them were in favor of MHFA's style of operation. Second, MHFA, unlike the other agencies studied, did not deal directly with the public; instead it was buffered by developers, banks, and local housing agencies.

The nature of MHFA's task also helped insulate it from any attempt by the governor to change its behavior. The criteria for success—building new housing while remaining financially solvent—were clear. As long as MHFA was able to achieve these goals, which also worked in Sargent's favor, there was no need for him to expend scarce resources he needed for handling crises to change the agency's behavior.[5] White shrewdly resisted the governor's offers to allow his agency to take on more functions, such as development, that would have made the measure of the agency's success more problematic. The public environment in which the agency operated was both limited and favorable to the way the agency was running. Because the agency financed large numbers of housing units, dealt with a highly technical subject, and had a powerful and vocal constituency, Sargent never felt a need to attempt to change its behavior, nor was he called on to do so.

The Department of Mental Health, unlike MHFA and DPW, had no single definable task or objective. As in the DPW, the department's mission was changing during Sargent's term. Unlike Public Works, however, the department's mission was changing not because of opposition to a particular issue but because of general, widely diffused support for a program of uncertain dimensions. Neither the public nor Sargent perceived any single crisis issue. There was support for moving people out of institutions, but no one knew what to do with them after that. The avowed goal of deinstitutionalizing the mentally ill while improving their mental health required a technology and a method of proceeding that no one in the department or outside it was able to identify.

Management of DMH was especially difficult not only because of the lack of clarity of the department's goals but also because of the environment in which it operated. As with the Department of Public Welfare, support for any single Mental Health initiative was diffuse. The most powerful of its new constituents were those who opposed something the department was currently doing rather than those who had proposals for the direction that the department should take. Like the DPW, DMH's management was dominated by professionals. Unlike the engineers in DPW, however, the psychiatrists in DMH did not have a strong notion of a hierarchical chain of command; instead they demanded autonomy in making both professional and administrative decisions.

The fact that criteria for success were so hard to define and that support for any single policy was diffuse made DMH difficult for a governor or anyone else to manage. Sargent's inclination to avoid managing DMH was reinforced by the fact that the public "incidents" and "crises" involving the department during his term occurred far less frequently than they did, for example, in public welfare. Public concern over mental health, though widespread, was not so intense or so focused on one goal that he could not afford to ignore the department as much as possible and in so doing avoid the enormous cost in resources and political support that any initiative on his part might have entailed.

Implications for Public Policy

Traditional democratic theory has provided a flawed model of administrative management of the public sector. Agencies are not always responsive to either the chief executive or the electorate. And governors do not always listen to or understand the wishes of the electorate on issues of public policy. Perhaps the most important, though most obvious, conclusion of this study is that in order to ensure some form of governmental accountability we need to have more realistic and more precise expectations about what management of public bureaucracies means. This study has shown that there are several problems with the "conventional wisdom" of public management. These can be recapitulated simply.

The most important factor that conditions the extent to which a governor attempts to intervene in agency affairs is his perception of the presence or absence of crisis. He is not totally in control of his agenda. He cannot devote much of his time to planning or to affecting policy from its inception to its implementation. At the same time, no elected chief executive can afford to muddle through or only attempt to affect policy at the margins. He must respond to issues that are placed on his agenda by forces outside his own control. At best, the political executive can appear to cover these crises by calculating an intervention at the appropriate time and by identifying himself closely with those issues that lend themselves to some sort of successful resolution. How successful he is at managing the process of making sound public policy depends less on his own calculations of what that policy should be and how it should be carried out than on his ability to discriminate among crises and on his willingness to balance his agenda to accommodate to long-term as well as short-term crises.

Although all governors must spend large amounts of time dealing with crises, they do not all manage the executive branch the same way. They have different styles, different interests, and different resources. They are constrained in their ability to manage, though the constraints and ways to get around them may vary from governor to governor and from one period of time to another. "Public management," even "crisis management," involves not one task, but many. Therefore, it makes sense that the public should recognize that the important question to ask about a governor is not "How good is he at management?" but instead, "What kind of management needs to be done and what kind of elected manager does this call for?" For example, if there is a publicly felt need for dramatic initiation of new policies, it might be important for the electorate to select an "advocate governor" who has a series of issues he wants placed on his own agenda and who is willing publicly to take the lead on them. If, on the other hand, the public feels that government is not running properly because the administrative apparatus is in need of long-range change, the electorate should look for a different kind of chief executive, one who is good at identifying and encouraging the development of technocratic or bureaucratic issues and who is willing to give them a prominent place on his agenda. Finally, if the nature of the political climate is such that the major issue concerning the elec-

torate is that government does not respond to popular sentiment, perhaps the kind of elected manager they should be looking for is one whose style and temperament are geared to responding quickly and conscientiously to public opinion.
We also know that, despite what organization charts lead us to
believe, the accountability of agencies to the governor and to
the public varies. Sometimes governors or their designees set
agency agendas. Their interest in doing this usually varies according to the agencies' crisis potential. Sometimes these
agendas are set by constituents, by professional groups, or by
the agency personnel themselves in accordance with the methods they have developed for handling their business. The important implication of this for public policy is that the question of
how accountable an agency is to a governor is not always the
appropriate question to ask in attempting to find out how well
it serves a public purpose. Instead, the important questions to
ask are those that discriminate both among agencies and among
their policies. All agencies should not be accountable to governors all the time because, by virtue of their being elected, governors cannot handle certain important administrative functions
such as a variety of noncrisis, "nuts and bolts" management
issues. The important questions then become, given the task or
tasks of an agency, how far should it be removed from having to
respond instantly to public opinion or to a governor's perception of public opinion? What questions should be left in the
hands of the political system, the electorate, and the governor
to be "managed" and which ones should be delegated to professional managers who are not directly accountable to any part of
the political system?

Beyond asking more realistic questions about governors and
about their administrative agencies, it is important to understand and to take into account the limitations inherent in the
idea of public management in assessing what expectations for
improvement of the quality of government it is reasonable to
hold. Americans have always been optimistic in their belief that
government is within the grasp of the common people and that

people can be trained to understand what government is doing and, to a lesser extent, how government may be controlled. In recent years, this optimism has been directed toward the possibility of training government managers. It is clear from this study that there are some things managers can be taught'that will aid them in managing. They can be helped to develop the "situational resources" they may be called upon to use. For example, they can be trained to understand formal and informal authority, to develop skills that will allow them to define a task more clearly, to understand the history and political climate of a given jurisdiction, and to develop the technical expertise necessary to deal with a particular problem. Although this training may be useful, it is certainly not a panacea. The problems of management are not homogeneous or predictable and each one calls for a different ordering of skills. In addition, as Edward Banfield has pointed out, successful management is as much an art as a science, and it is difficult to teach because how it can be accomplished is not subject to fixed rules.[6]

A second problem inherent in the notion of public management is that although one of the primary difficulties in running public agencies is lack of clarity or diffusion of tasks, there are few incentives for anyone in the political system to take the initiative to define clearly what the management tasks are. To the extent that these tasks are clearly defined and public, they provide measures for success or failure. Agencies and governors do not want to make explicit their measures of success for agencies on which the public places a variety of demands. By doing so they would set up clear criteria to measure their success or failure and risk alienating the public to which they are ultimately responsible by choosing to limit the agenda of those agencies. Even interest groups run a risk if they publicly make their goals clear and specific because they are demanding particular goods from organizations that are supposed to serve the general public interest. Management implies the setting of explicit goals, but implicit in the notion of public management is the idea that the debate over what these goals should be is open to the public.

There are no incentives in the political system for resolving what these goals should be if there is widespread disagreement over them. Instead, public managers must work in a system in which the best way to ensure that an issue is dealt with is to figure out how to declare it to be a "crisis." One of the possible methods of improving public sector management and one of the points on which citizen concern should be focused is identifying what incentives can be provided to encourage individuals at all levels of the political system to define more clearly and more precisely what they want the short- and long-run tasks of administrative agencies to be.

This leads to perhaps the most serious difficulty inherent in public management. The fact that management of agencies occurs in a political environment means that both governors and agencies must be subject to two different notions of accountability. To the extent that they are part of the political system, both are supposed to be "accountable" to the public by being responsive to them. This kind of accountability often clashes with the more conventional notion of private sector accountability, which prescribes that agencies should have explicit fixed goals, follow set procedures for achieving them, and be evaluated according to whether they accomplish what they set out to do.

In the public sector, these two notions of accountability lead to an insoluble problem for both the chief executive and the organizations he must manage. To the extent that agencies respond to public demands for exceptions to rules and for special favors, they are accountable to someone other than the chief executive. To the extent that they behave as he explicitly orders them to do, or as the personnel of the agency think he would like them to behave, they often do not respond to the public's demands.

Governors, too, face this dilemma. As managers they have a responsibility to set goals for their organizations and to deal with the issues bureaucrats raise. At the same time, as elected officials they are accountable to the public and have to deal with the issues the public places on their agenda, whether these displace issues already there or work explicitly against those goals they have already set.

Governors and their ability to manage the agencies for which they are responsible vary from state to state and from one period of time to another. But it is clear that because governors and agencies operate in the public sector, because their attention must be devoted to crisis management, and because they are evaluated by the peculiar set of management standards the public generates, their operations and problems are more alike than they are different. They all fall victim to the often conflicting criteria for performance that the public has for them. Whether the problems for public management these conflicting demands cause can themselves be managed depends both on the ability of the public to be taught or to change its expectations of what political executives should do and on whether the public can become sufficiently discriminating to identify which issues should be handled immediately by the political system and which ones should be managed for them by an administrative system that will not always be instantly responsive.

Notes

1

For a more detailed description of the "rational actor" model and the "muddling through" model, see Herbert Simon, *Administrative Behavior* and Charles Lindblom, "The Science of Muddling Through." Graham Allison's book *Essence of Decision, Explaining the Cuban Missile Crisis* provides an excellent summary of the literature on decision making.

2

An excellent analysis of this kind of calculation has been done by Edward Banfield in his book, *Political Influence.*

3

It is well known that decisions are often made in the lower levels of organizations without having been explicitly delegated. One of the cornerstones of the theory of the incrementalists is that decisionmakers give limited attention to a small number of specific tasks and that major decisions are often made because of the operating procedures of lower levels of their organizations. As Graham Allison describes this phenomenon in *Essence of Decision,* "Individual subunits of the organization handle pieces of the firm's separated problem in relative independence. Inconsistency that occurs as a result of this "local rationality" is absorbed by organizational slack" (p. 76).

The implicit assumption of much of this literature is that this kind of delegation by default is a serious limitation on the executive and is something that he would remedy if he could. In fact, this is not always the case.

4

Paul Lawrence and Jay Lorsch, *Organization and Environment: Managing Differentiation and Integration.*

5

The importance of financial solvency to freedom from gubernatorial intervention was dramatically illustrated in early 1976 when, because of the instability of the municipal bond market, MHFA had difficulty in selling its bonds. Governor Michael Dukakis and his staff became heavily involved immediately in the finances of the agency and set up a high-level task force to look at MHFA management.

6

Edward Banfield, "The Training of the Executive." It may be useful in thinking about the possibility of training public managers to distinguish between knowledge of a substantive area, which can be taught, and skill, which one could argue is a product of experience and natural talent.

Selected Bibliography

Allison, Graham. *Essence of Decision, Explaining the Cuban Missile Crisis.* Boston: Little, Brown and Co., 1971.

Andrews, Kenneth. *The Concept of Corporate Strategy.* Homewood, Ill.: Dow Jones-Irwin, 1971.

Bailis, Larry. "Bread or Justice: Grassroots Organizing in the Welfare Rights Movement." Ph.D. dissertation, Harvard University, 1972.

Banfield, Edward. *Political Influence.* New York: The Free Press, 1961.

_____. "The Training of the Executive." In *Public Policy*, vol. X, edited by Carl Friedrich and Seymour Harris. Cambridge, Mass.: Graduate School of Public Administration, Harvard University, 1960.

Barnard, Chester. *The Functions of the Executive.* Cambridge, Mass.: Harvard University Press, 1971.

Buck, A. E. *The Reorganization of State Governments in the United States.* New York: Columbia University Press, 1938.

Citizens Housing and Planning Association of Metropolitan Boston. *All in Together, A Report on Income Mixing in Multifamily Housing.* Boston: CHPA, 1974.

Commission on the Organization of the Executive Branch of Government. "General Management of the Executive Branch." A Report to the Congress. February, 1949.

Crozier, Michel. *The Bureaucratic Phenomenon.* Chicago, Ill.: University of Chicago Press, 1964.

Cyert, R., and March, J. *A Behavioral Theory of the Firm.* Englewood Cliffs, N.J.: Prentice Hall, 1963.

Derthick, Martha. *The Influence of Federal Grants, Public Assistance in Massachusetts.* Cambridge, Mass.: Harvard University Press, 1970.

Dimock, Marshall. *A Philosophy of Administration.* New York: Harper, 1958.

Edelman, Murray. *The Symbolic Uses of Politics.* Urbana, Ill.: The University of Illinois Press, 1964.

Fenno, Richard. "The House Committee on Education and Labor." In *Readings in Congress*, edited by Raymond Wolfinger. Englewood Cliffs, N.J.: Prentice Hall, 1971.

_____. "The House Appropriations Committee as a Political System: The Problem of Integration." *American Political Science Review*, 56 (1962).

Final Report of the Special Commission on Low Income Housing. Massachusetts House No. 4040, April, 1965.

Fox, Douglas. *The Politics of City and State Bureaucracy.* Pacific Palisades, Calif.: Goodyear Publishing, 1974.

Friedman, Robert S. "State Politics and Highways." In *Politics in the American States,* edited by Herbert Jacob and Kenneth Vines. Boston: Little, Brown and Co., 1965.

F.Y. *'75 Budget: Summary of Programs and Recommendations or the Budget in English.* Boston: Commonwealth of Massachusetts, 1974.

Gakenheimer, Ralph. *Transportation Planning as Response to Controversy: Participation and Conflict in the Boston Case.* Cambridge, Mass.: The M.I.T. Press, 1975.

Grob, Gerald. *The State and the Mentally Ill.* Chapel Hill, N.C.: University of North Carolina Press, 1966.

Hamberg, Charles. "Mental Health as a Government Service." Ph.D. dissertation, Harvard University, 1957.

Hitch, Charles, and McKean, Roland. *The Economics of Defense in the Nuclear Age.* Cambridge, Mass.: Harvard University Press, 1960.

Holden, Matthew. "Imperialism in Bureaucracy." In *The National Administrative System, Selected Readings.* Edited by Dean Yarwood. New York: Wiley, 1971.

Johnson, Richard T. "Management Styles of Three U.S. Presidents," Stanford Business School Alumni *Bulletin,* Fall, 1973.

Lawrence, Paul, and Lorsch, Jay. *Organization and Environment: Managing Differentiation and Integration.* Boston: Division of Research, Graduate School of Business Administration, Harvard University, 1967.

Lindblom, Charles. "The Science of Muddling Through." In *Public Administration,* edited by Robert Golembiewski, Frank Gibson, and Geoffrey Cornog. 2nd ed. Chicago: Rand McNally, 1972.

Lipson, Leslie. *The American Governor from Figurehead to Leader.* Chicago, Ill.: University of Chicago Press, 1939.

Litt, Edgar. *The Political Cultures of Massachusetts.* Cambridge, Mass.: The MIT Press, 1965.

"Living Together: Massachusetts Tries Mixing Income Groups in Subsidized Housing." *Wall Street Journal,* June 25, 1974.

Lupo, Alan; Colcord, Frank; and Fowler, Edmund P. *Rites of Way: The Politics of Transportation in Boston and the U.S. City.* Boston: Little, Brown and Co., 1971.

MacDonald, Austin F. *American State Government and Administration.* 5th ed. New York: Crowell, 1955.

Massachusetts Housing Finance Agency. "First Annual Report." Mimeographed. Boston: MHFA, 1969.

National Study Service. *Meeting the Problems of People in Massachusetts, A Study of the Massachusetts Public Welfare System.* Boston: The Massachusetts Committee on Children and Youth, 1966.

Neustadt, Richard. *Presidential Power.* New York: Signet, 1960.

Pressman, Jeffrey. "Preconditions of Mayoral Leadership." *American Political Science Review* 66(1972):511-524.

Ransone, Coleman. *The Office of Governor in the United States.* Tuscaloosa, Ala.: University of Alabama Press, 1956.

Report of the Massachusetts Mental Hospital Planning Project. Boston: United Community Planning Council, 1974.

Robbins, Robert, ed. *State Government and Public Responsibility: The Role of the Governor in Massachusetts.* Papers of the 1961 Tufts Assembly on Massachusetts Government. Medford, Mass.: Tufts University, 1961.

Schick, Allen. *Budget Innovation in the States.* Washington: The Brookings Institution, 1971.

Seidman, Harold. *Politics, Position and Power.* New York: Oxford University Press, 1970.

Selznick, Philip. *Leadership in Administration.* Evanston, Ill.: Row, Peterson, 1957.

Simon, Herbert. *Administrative Behavior.* 2nd ed. New York: The Macmillan Co., 1957.

Task Force on Children Out of School. *Suffer the Children.* Boston, Mass.: Task Force on Children Out of School, 1972.

Turrett, J. Stephen. "The Vulnerability of American Governors, 1900-1969." *Midwest Journal of Political Science*, 15 (1971), No. 1.

Willbern, York. "Administration in State Governments." In *The American Assembly. The Forty-eight States: Their Tasks as Policy Makers and Administrators.* New York: Columbia University Press, 1955.

Wilson, James Q. *Varieties of Police Behavior.* New York: Atheneum, 1972.

Wood, Robert C. "The Metropolitan Governor—Three Inquiries into the Substance of State Executive Management." Ph.D. dissertation, Harvard University, 1949.

Wright, Deil. "Executive Leadership in State Administration." *Midwest Journal of Political Science,* 11 (1967), No. 1.

Young, James Sterling. *The Washington Community 1800-1828.* New York: Columbia University Press, 1966.

Index

Accelerated Highway Act of 1972, 79
Administration and Finance, Executive Office of, 60, 98, 170
Agencies
control of, 9-13, 220-225
defined, 9
variations in, 11-13
Agencies, variations in, 8-11, 66-70, 210, 218-225, 227
Agenda-setting, 50-58, 219, 220
variations in, 51
Agnew, Spiro, 46
Agriculture, Massachusetts Department of, 69
Agriculture, U.S. Department of, 113
Aid to the Blind, category of welfare, 126
Aid to Families with Dependent Children (AFDC), 112. *See also* Social Security Act of 1935
Allison, Graham, 231n1, 231n3
Altshuler, Alan, 86, 87, 91-102, 104n17, 104n21, 105n24, 105n26, 105n28, 140, 217, 222
management, style of, 91-102
relationship to Sargent, 96-102
Andrews, Kenneth, 21, 40n3, 40n4, 40n5, 72n9
Association for Mentally Ill Children (AMIC), 186

Bailis, Lawrence, 145n26
Banfield, Edward, 228, 231n2, 231n6
Barnard, Chester, 22, 40n6
Beer, Samuel, 71n5
Belchertown State School for the Retarded, 191, 192, 198, 199, 200, 201
deaths at, 192, 201, 202
Bloomberg, Wilfred, 201, 206n15
Boone, John, 55, 72n8
Boston, City of, 49, 133
Sargent dealings with, 49
Boston State Hospital, 189
Boston Transportation Planning Review (BTPR), 94, 95, 97
Bridwell, Lowell, 84

Campbell, Bruce, 91-95, 98-101, 104n22, 104n23
Chapter 735, the Comprehensive Mental Health and Retardation Services Act of 1963, 180, 191
Charities, State Board of, 179
Child Guardianship, Division of, of the Department of Public Welfare, 112
Children, Office for, 56, 116
Children's Defense Fund, 116
Citizens Housing and Planning Association, 175n2, 176n19
Civil Service, Massachusetts, 36, 78, 79, 82, 115, 125, 183
Colcord, Frank, 72n7, 104n11, 104n13, 104n14, 104n15
Collins, John, 83
Commerce and Development, Executive Office of, 166, 167
Community Affairs, Department of (DCA), 68, 151, 152, 154, 167-169, 171-173
Community Mental Health Centers Act (U.S.) of 1963, 180
Comprehensive Mental Health and Retardation Services Act of 1963 (Chapter 735), 180, 191
Conway, Jerry, 104n19
Corporations and Taxation, Department of, 152
Corrections, Department of, 55, 67

Crampton, Lewis, 168, 176n18,
176n22
Crisis Management, 7, 8, 50, 54, 68,
209-220, 222-226, 230
costs of, 57, 58
effect on staff of, 65, 66
in Department of Mental Health,
197, 198, 203, 204
in Department of Public Welfare,
124-128, 131, 132, 139, 141,
142
in Department of Public Works,
86-89
in Massachusetts Housing Finance
Agency, 165, 172
in Sargent administration, 25, 26,
50, 54, 86-89, 96, 101, 102,
124-128, 131, 132, 139, 141,
142, 165, 172, 197, 198, 203,
204
"Critical environments," 221

Daniels, Russell, 198-202, 206n16,
216
Davoren, John, 132
Decisionmaking, 6-8, 50, 54, 68,
209-220
crisis management model, 7, 8,
50, 54, 68, 209-220
"muddling through" model, 7, 8,
210-212, 214-219
rational policymaker model, 7, 8,
210-213, 215, 216, 218, 219
Deinstitutionalization, 68, 190,
195, 198, 211-213, 224
Derthick, Martha, 115, 118, 143n4,
143n6, 143n7, 144n14
Dever, Paul, 68
Dimock, Marshall, 14n4
Disability Assistance (DA), category of welfare, 112, 126
Dix, Dorothea, 179
Drew, John, 19, 135, 136

Dukakis, Michael, 10, 41n10,
144n15, 200, 231n5
Dumont, Robert, 18, 35, 42n15
Dwight, Donald, 17, 27, 37, 38, 85,
86
Dye, Thomas, 72n10

Edelman, Murray, 71n4
Employment Security, Division of,
63, 69
Eskind, Robert, 171, 176n23
Executives, chief, job of public
compared to job of private,
21-24

Family and Children's Services,
proposed state Department
of, 138
Federal Aid Road Act of 1916, 77
Federal Highway Act of 1944, 77
Federal Highway Act of 1956, 77
Federal Highway Administration
(FHWA), of the U.S. Depart-
ment of Transportation, 80,
114
Federal Housing Administration
(FHA), 150
Feeley, Frank, R., 143n5
Fenno, Richard, 14n6
Fiscal Affairs, Office of, of the
Executive Office of Adminis-
tration and Finance, 170, 171
Fitzpatrick, John, 72n8
Flannery, Jack, 17, 18, 27, 28, 33,
34, 36, 41n11, 42n16
"Flat grant" policy, in the Depart-
ment of Public Welfare, 132,
134-136, 140, 211, 213
Ford, Friendly, 205n9
Fowler, Edmund, 72n7, 104n11,
104n13, 104n14, 104n15
Fox, Douglas, 72n10
Frank, Barney, 86

Friedman, Robert, 103n1
Friends of the Belchertown State
    School, 199, 200
Funkhauser, Hope, 176n15

Gakenheimer, Ralph, 104n11
Gardner State Hospital, 179
General Court. *See* Legislature,
    Massachusetts
General Relief (GR), category of
    welfare, 112
Glynn, Thomas, 176n21, 176n24
Goldman, William, 193, 194, 202,
    206n14
Goldmark, Peter, 27, 41n13, 190-
    192, 198-202, 206n13, 216
Gorsky, William, 205n2
Governor Sargent Committees, 46
Governors
    as chief executive officers, 20-39
    criteria for evaluation of, 2, 226,
        227
    roles played by, 45-50
    theories of accountability of, 3,
        225, 226, 229, 230
    variation in behavior of, 8, 226,
        227, 229, 230
Governor's Appointments Office,
    18
Governor's Office, structure of,
    under Sargent, 18, 19
Governor's Office of Service, 18
Governor's Office of State Service,
    18, 36, 166, 167
Governor's Task Force on Trans-
    portation, 86, 87, 91, 94
Greater Boston Coalition (GBC),
    84, 86
Greenblatt, Milton, 188-192, 201,
    202, 206n13, 217
Grob, Gerald, 205n1

Hamberg, Charles, 205n1

Health, Education and Welfare,
    U.S. Department of (HEW),
    113, 114
Hertz, George, 205n4, 205n7
Highway construction, controversy
    over, 84-89, 92, 94, 95, 97,
    98, 100, 101
Highway Maintenance Account, 80
Hill-Burton Act, for hospital con-
    struction, 182
Hitch, Charles, 14n4
Hobbs, Matthew, 175n11
Holden, Matthew, 176n13
Hoover Commission report, "Com-
    mission on the Organization
    of the Executive Branch,"
    14n3, 40n1
Housing and Urban Development
    (HUD), U.S. Department of,
    153, 154, 166
Hughes, Jane, 206n16
Human Services, Executive Office
    of, 57, 109, 116, 189, 199,
    200, 205n5
Humphrey, Tom, 104n20

I-93 (interstate highway), 84, 89
I-95 (interstate highway), 84, 89
Inner Belt, highway, Greater Bos-
    ton, 84, 87, 89, 94
Insanity, State Board of, 179

Johnson, Richard, 72n11
Joseph, George, 103n6, 103n7

Kennedy, John, F., President, 180
Kershner, Joel, 176n22
Klebanoff, Elton, 56
Klein, Andrew, 56
Kramer, Albert, 17, 19, 25-28, 32-
    34, 41n9, 47, 55, 57, 86, 96,
    97, 135, 136

Lawrence, Paul, 40n2, 221, 231n4
Leadership, 4, 5, 44, 66, 208
  gubernatorial, why study, 5
  variations in, 44, 66, 208
Legislature, Massachusetts (also
    known as the General Court),
    38, 47, 48, 59, 79-81, 90,
    110, 117-119, 120, 121, 126,
    130-133, 150-152, 162-164,
    170, 171, 180, 184, 185, 189,
    193
  House Committee on Ways and
    Means of, 38, 59
  relationship with Department of
    Mental Health, 180, 184, 185,
    189, 193
  relationship with Department of
    Public Welfare, 110, 117-119,
    120, 121, 126, 130-133
  relationship with Department of
    Public Works, 79-81, 90
  relationship with MHFA, 150-
    152, 162-164, 170, 171
  relationship with Sargent, 47, 48
  Senate Ways and Means, 38
Levitta, Bernie, 103n5
Lidell, Charles, 144n12, 145n21
Liederman, David, 136
Lindblom, Charles, 7, 14n5, 231n1
Lindsay, John, 190
Linsky, Martin, 41n12, 136
Lorsch, Jay, 40n2, 221, 231n4
Low Income Housing, Massachu-
    setts Special Commission on,
    150, 175n1
Lunacy and Charities, State Board
    of, 179
Lupo, Alan, 72n7, 104n11,
    104n13, 104n14, 104n15

McKean, Roland, 14n4
McLaughlin, Richard, 201
Management, public
  compared to private sector man-
    agement, 6, 20-24, 39, 221
  conventional wisdom about, 6,
    220, 225
  limitations inherent in:
    task definition, 228, 229
    training, 227, 228
    variation in accountability, 229
  meaning of, 4
    for governors, 3
  tasks implied in, 24-39
    allocating resources, 24, 37-39
    changing or initiating policy,
      24, 26-29
    maintaining positions, 24, 29,
      30
    marketing, 24, 33-35
    mediating disputes, 24, 32, 33
    recruiting, 24, 35-37
    setting a tone, 24, 31, 32
Mann, Horace, 179
Martin, David, 157
Massachusetts, budget of, 16
Massachusetts, employees of, 16
Massachusetts Advocacy Center,
    186
Massachusetts Association for
    Learning Disabilities, 186
Massachusetts Association for Men-
    tal Health, 186, 190
Massachusetts Association for Re-
    tarded Citizens (MARC), 186,
    187
Massachusetts Bay Transportation
    Authority (MBTA), 149
Massachusetts Committee on Chil-
    dren and Youth, 186
Massachusetts Housing Finance
    Agency (MHFA), 11, 12, 69,
    148-174, 214, 217, 220, 223,
    224
  background and description of,
    150-156

constituents of, 162-165
funding of, 148, 152-154, 167,
168, 171
norms of behavior in, 155, 156,
159, 160
organization of, 148, 149, 151,
152
personnel of, 148, 154-156, 158,
160, 161
relationship to DCA, 167-169
relationship to federal government, 153, 154
relationship to legislature, 150-
152, 162-164, 170, 171
relationship of Office of Fiscal
Affairs, 169-172
task of, 156-159, 162, 169, 174,
223
Massachusetts Law Reform Institute, 17
Massachusetts Mental Health Center, 189
Massachusetts Mental Health Hospital Planning Project, 205n1,
205n3
Massachusetts Port Authority, 69,
149, 172, 173, 215
Massachusetts Turnpike Authority,
149
Massachusetts Welfare Rights
Organization, 134
Master Highway Plan of 1948, 84
Medicaid, 111, 112, 121, 124, 182.
See also Social Security Act
of 1935
Mental Health, Department of
(DMH), 11, 12, 68, 178-204,
213, 215, 220, 223-225
area boards of, 181, 186, 189,
191, 192, 194
background and description of,
178-187
change of mission in, 178, 187,
188, 195-197, 224

constituencies of, 184-187, 191,
197, 198
funding of, 181-183
organization of, 179-184
personnel of, 183, 184
professionalism in, 183-186, 188,
196, 197, 224
relationship with courts, 191
relationship with federal government, 180, 182
relationship with legislature, 180,
184, 185, 189, 193
reorganization of 1969, 189
task of, 178, 187, 188, 195, 196,
198, 202, 224
Mental Illness and Health, Joint
Congressional Commission
on, 180
Metropolitan District Commission,
36
Miller, Jerome, 30
Minter, Steven, 30, 72n8, 122-125,
127-131, 136-141, 144n10,
144n19, 145n22, 145n23,
216, 217
management style of, 122-131,
137, 138, 140
Mintzberg, Henry, 40n2
Moriarty, Ricki, 176n21
Morrow, William, 19, 47
Mystic River Bridge, collapse of,
100

National Housing Act, section 236
of, 153
National Institutes of Health, 182
National Study Service, 120,
143n1, 144n17
National Welfare Rights Organization, 122
Natural Resources, Department of,
16, 17, 36
Neustadt, Richard, 4, 14n1, 58,
72n9

New York City Budget Bureau, 190
New York State Housing Finance
　　Authority, 150
"The Nine Year Old in Norfolk
　　Prison," WTIC documentary,
　　199
Nixon, Richard, 46, 48
　　administration of, 48, 114

Ogilvie, Richard, 41n10, 51
Old Age Assistance (OAA), cate-
　　gory of welfare, 112, 126
O'Leary, Daniel, 103n1
Olver, John, 200
Ott, Robert, 72n8, 121, 122, 124,
　　133, 135, 140, 143n5,
　　145n25

Park Plaza Redevelopment Project,
　　68
Peabody, Endicott, 18, 121, 150
Peabody, Malcolm, 150
Pressman, Jeffrey, 14n6
Public Health, Department of, 57,
　　67
Public Roads, Bureau of, of the
　　Federal Highway Administra-
　　tion, 80
Public Welfare, Department of, 11,
　　12, 55, 63, 67, 108-142, 148,
　　165, 182, 195, 202, 213, 214,
　　217-220, 222-224
　　background and description of,
　　　109-120
　　categorical programs of, 110-113,
　　　124, 126
　　constituents of, 116-119, 122,
　　　130, 131
　　"flat grant policy," 132, 134-136,
　　　140, 211, 213
　　funding of, 109, 111-113, 118,
　　　124, 126, 132
　　organization of, 109-112, 120

personnel of, 114-117, 125, 129,
　　130, 135, 136
professionalism in, 115-117, 129,
　　130
relationship with federal govern-
　　ment, 110, 112-115, 124-126,
　　128, 129, 136, 137
relationship with legislature, 110,
　　117-119, 120, 121, 126, 130-
　　133
reorganization proposal for 1972,
　　126, 132, 137-140
separation of eligibility from ser-
　　vices, 132, 136, 137
state takeover of, 111, 115, 120-
　　122, 126, 132-134
tasks of, 108, 119, 120, 139, 222
Public Works, Department of
　　(DPW), 11, 12, 17, 67, 76-
　　102, 108, 113, 114, 131, 140,
　　148, 165, 178, 183, 187, 195,
　　196, 198, 219-224
　　background and development of,
　　　76-82
　　change of mission in, 83-96, 101,
　　　102, 221
　　funding of, 79, 80
　　management of, 82-102
　　norms of behavior in, 76, 81, 82,
　　　87, 88, 90, 94, 101
　　organization of, 77, 78, 81, 82
　　personnel of, 78, 79, 81, 82, 90,
　　　101, 102
　　professionalism in, 81, 82, 90,
　　　92-95, 101
　　relationship with federal govern-
　　　ment, 77, 79, 80, 84, 89, 90,
　　　99
　　relationship with legislature, 79-
　　　81, 90
　　task of, 94, 95, 101, 102, 221

Quinn, Robert, 48

Reardon, Thomas, 18, 19, 34
Republican Party, 46, 48
Resources, 58-66, 149, 173, 174,
    208, 228
  enabling, 63-66
  personal, 58, 59
  situational, 59-63, 228
Ribbs, Edward, 72n8, 83-88, 91,
    101, 103n10, 104n12
Ricci, Benjamin, 191, 199, 200
Ricci v. Greenblatt, 191, 206n12
Richardson, Elliot, 114
Roslanowick, Jeanne, 144n11
Route 2, extension of, 87
Rowland, Richard, 143n3, 144n16,
    144n20, 145n27
Russell, William, 77
Ryan, John, 175n4
Ryoff, Steven, 176n16, 176n22

Salvucci, Fred, 103n9
Sargent, Francis, Governor, 6, 10-
    13, 16-21, 24, 25, 27-39,
    40n7, 41n8, 41n10, 44-51,
    54-57, 59-65, 67-69, 76, 78,
    82, 83-88, 92, 96, 97, 99-
    102, 108-110, 121-125, 132-
    141, 148, 149, 155, 156,
    159-161, 163-167, 170, 172-
    174, 178, 188, 190, 192-204,
    206n18, 208, 210-217, 219-
    225
  background of, 16, 60, 61, 76
  campaigns of
    1970, 59, 86, 122, 123, 135
    1974, 10, 172
  formal authority of, 62, 148,
    149, 165, 166
  management style of, 16-19, 24-
    39, 44-66, 202-204
  recruiting, 35-37
  use of budgetary skills and con-
    trols, 37-39, 62, 170-172
  policy initiatives of, 54, 57, 68,
    134-139
  as political campaigner, 45, 46
  relationship with legislature, 47,
    48
  relationship with Republican
    Party, 46, 48
  role in highway controversy, 85-
    89
  staff of, 17-19, 56, 57, 64-66,
    135, 136, 166
  use of resources by, 58-66, 173,
    174
Sarsfield, Edward, 205n7
Sattenstein, Leon, 143n8, 143n9
Schick, Allen, 42n18
Seidman, Harold, 40n1
Selznick, Philip, 22, 40n6
Simon, Herbert, 14n4, 231n1
Singer, Dorothy, 143n5
Social and Rehabilitation Service
    (SRS), of the U.S. Depart-
    ment of Health, Education
    and Welfare, 113
Social Security Act of 1935, 110,
    182
  categorical provisions of
    Aid to Families with Dependent
      Children (AFDC), 112
    disabled (DA), 110
    Medicaid, 111, 112
    medically indigent (MAA), 110
    medicare, 182
    Supplemental Security Income,
      182
Solomon, Harry, 188
Southeast Expressway, 87
"Special needs" grants of welfare,
    135
"State Care Acts," for DMH, 205n6
Suffer the Children, report of the
    Task Force on Children Out
    of School, 190, 206n10

Supreme Judicial Court of Massa-
  chusetts, 151
Task Force on Children Out of
  School, 186, 190, 206n10
Technocratic issues, 52, 53, 219
Teichner, Stephen, 19, 34
"13-A" (state housing interest sub-
  sidy program), 154
Tierney, Robert, 82, 94, 103n3,
  103n4, 103n8, 104n18
Transportation and Construction,
  Executive Office of, 96, 98,
  99
Transportation, Department of,
  U.S., 80, 89

Urban Development Corporation of
  New York, 159
Urban Mass Transit Administration
  of the U.S. Department of
  Transportation, 89
Urban Planning Aid, 84
U.S. Outdoor Recreation Resources
  Review Commission, 16
Uyterhoeven, Hugo, 40n2

Volpe, John, 16-18, 28, 76, 83, 85,
  121, 132-134, 140, 151, 166,
  188

Weiner, Stephen, 29, 56, 57
White, Kevin, Mayor, 17, 49, 59,
  86, 132
White, William, 157-159, 161, 162,
  165, 166, 172, 175n7, 175n9,
  175n10, 176n12, 176n17,
  176n20, 217, 224
  management style of, 157-163
Wilson, James Q., 14n7
Wofford, John, 97, 105n27
Wood, Robert, 40n1, 49, 71n3
Worcester State Hospital, 179
Wrapp, Edward, 40n2
Wyatt v. Stickney, 191, 206n11

Yasi, Robert, 17, 18
Young, James Sterling, 4, 14n2,
  72n9
Young, William, 19
Youth Services, Department of, 30,
  126, 138